MAN ALIVE:
A PRIMER OF MEN'S ISSUES

FREDRIC E. RABINOWITZ

University of Redlands

SAM V. COCHRAN

University of Iowa

Brooks/Cole Publishing Company
Pacific Grove, California

I(**T**)**P**™ The trademark ITP is used under license.

A CLAIREMONT BOOK

Brooks/Cole Publishing Company
A Division of Wadsworth, Inc.

Printed in the United States of America
10 9 8 7 6 5 4 3 2 1

Library of Congress Cataloging-in-Publication Data
Rabinowitz, Fredric Eldon.
    Man alive : a primer of men's issues / by Fredric E. Rabinowitz
and Sam V. Cochran.
        p.   cm.
    Includes bibliographical references and index.
    ISBN 0-534-21792-3
    1. Men—Psychology.   2. Gay men—Psychology.   3. Man-woman
relationships.   4. Interpersonal relations.   5. Male friendship.
I. Cochran, Sam Victor, [date].   II. Title.
HQ1090.R33   1994
305.32—dc20   93-28043
                                                     CIP

Sponsoring Editor: *Claire Verduin*
Marketing Representative: *Reita Kinsman*
Editorial Associate: *Gay C. Bond*
Production Editor: *Laurel Jackson*
Manuscript Editor: *Joanne Tenenbaum*
Permissions Editor: *Carline Haga*
Interior and Cover Design: *Katherine Minerva*
Cover Illustration: *Frank R. Blume*, painting of "The Screamer"
Photo Editor: *Diana Mara Henry*
Typesetting: *Kachina Typesetting, Inc.*
Printing and Binding: *Malloy Lithographing, Inc.*

Credits continue on page 187.

MAN ALIVE:
A PRIMER OF MEN'S ISSUES

TO OUR PARENTS,
SAM AND BOBBI RABINOWITZ AND SAM AND MARILYN COCHRAN,
WHO GAVE US ROOTS TO GROW AND WINGS TO FLY;
AND OUR DAUGHTERS, KATE COCHRAN AND KARINA RABINOWITZ,
WHO ARE TEACHING US THE MEANING OF GENERATIVITY

CONTENTS

PREFACE

WHY WE WROTE THIS BOOK

As two reasonably successful men struggling with how to be genuine, sensitive, and strong in our lives, we invite you to come with us on a journey of self-discovery. We believe that men are about to enter a renaissance of awareness and growth, extending past the roles we play as worker and provider, and allowing us to know ourselves more deeply. For many of us, our failure to understand how our inner emotional life works has motivated this quest for self-knowledge.

Like many of you, we have grown up in late 20th-century, American culture. We have been shaped by the same well-defined but rarely mentioned boundaries of what it means to be a man. The goal of this book is to provide an introduction to what has become known as "men's issues," to help you become aware of some of the unspoken rules that govern men's lives, and to help you change the aspects of your masculine identity that might be destructive to your mental, physical, and spiritual health.

In 1981, as graduate students, we began leading men's growth groups at the University of Missouri in Columbia. We were struck by how little attention was paid in both the professional and the popular press to the problems and conflicts encountered by men in America. Both of us devoured the sparse literature available on masculinity at the time, such as Goldberg's *The Hazards of Being Male* (1976), Fasteau's *The Male Machine* (1974), Pleck and Sawyer's *Men and Masculinity* (1974), and Farrell's *The Liberated Man* (1974). We were impressed by the issues these authors were bringing to consciousness. Among them were the male fear of appearing vulnerable, the lack of intimate communication between men, the ignoring of our health in our pursuit of money and power, the inability to express feelings, the need always to be in control regardless of the negative consequences, and our total reliance on intellect and reason at the expense of more intuitive modes of knowing. All these issues struck a deep chord within us.

Over the past 12 years, our men's groups have reflected the inherent contradictions in the traditional male role. Through genuine communication, we discovered that beneath a masculine facade of toughness and arrogance, were sensitive, hurting little boys who felt they had to be strong, unfeeling, and invulnerable to be accepted. Once the little boy was given permission to come forward and voice his feelings and thoughts, each man discovered a sense of acceptance and freedom that he had lost through years of socialization. Uncovering the inner self brought not only fear and pain, but also freedom, joy, and a continuing sense of vitality.

Much to our disappointment, for many men the decade of the 1980s was not an enlightened era. Fostered by an extremely narrow definition of masculine success, the problems related to male self-identity seemed to worsen. The ascendant values of the Reagan-Bush years led to the return of the cowboy stereotype and to a Rambo-like image of masculinity that defined the male psyche as a simplistic, achievement-oriented black box. The message for men during this period was "make money, be happy." The media role models of our culture continued to be powerful men in control— Donald Trump, Sylvester Stallone, Arnold Schwarzenegger, Ronald Reagan, and Mike Tyson. As metaphors of how to succeed in life, sports and warfare images were prominent male symbols of sacrifice and triumph in the workplace.

Although a visible minority of men were economically prosperous, most of us did not live up to the cultural ideals conveyed by the media. As male supermen, we felt we had to succeed in our careers, be dynamic lovers, and be sensitive to our families' needs. Because few of us were able to score highly in all areas of our lives, we were made to feel like failures by those we imagined were judging us. In reality, we probably judged ourselves more harshly than anyone else did.

Rather than express our frustration directly to those we loved, we often acted distant and became preoccupied with work, sporting events, or cars. For many men, a drink, a seat in front of the TV, and a dim awareness that something was wrong replaced the fantasy of ultimate success. Our denial of our feelings resulted in unexpected outbursts of anger at those we love and an inner deadness that covered up our loneliness and frustration.

This book is our response to the often destructive path that has been the accepted model of how to be a man. We are aware of how the equation for success has frequently become the pattern for a mask that hides our fears, conflicts, and ability to relate fully to those we love. This rigid model of masculinity keeps us looking for the perfect job, house, and partner to make us happy. But in the process, we avoid knowing ourselves and appreciating the riches within us. There are other pathways to creating a healthy masculine identity; we hope this book stimulates you to consider some of them.

WHO SHOULD READ THIS BOOK

We intend this book to be a guide for men of all ages to learn about and reflect on their own experience. It is designed for use in the classroom at both the undergraduate and graduate levels, in human service and helping skills training programs, and in other educational settings, such as professional seminars and workshops. It can also be used as a reference for agency libraries. In addition, this book is appropriate for use by therapists working with men in individual therapy and group settings. Women might also be interested in a book of this nature as they try to understand the men in their lives. Although the writing and exercises are geared toward men, women reading the book can alter the exercises and reinterpret the content to fit their own experience. We encourage you to debate and discuss the generalizations made about men and to express your own perspectives on the topic. In keeping with our emphasis on males, we have used the masculine pronoun throughout the book. We believe in the equality of the sexes; however, we feel that the content of this particular work lends itself best to the masculine pronoun.

We acknowledge those of you who are gay or bisexual and apologize for generalizing more about the heterosexual experience. We have tried to incorporate concerns and differences related to the gay male experience. To enhance this perspective, we recommend that you refer to the books listed in the chapter references and the suggested readings. To men of color, we also apologize for not articulating all the special concerns that come with growing up in diverse cultures. A whole book could be devoted to aspects of the cross-cultural male experience. Despite these shortcomings, we believe that many of the issues raised throughout the book will resonate with your experience as a male in North American culture.

WHAT YOU WILL FIND IN THIS BOOK

The chapters in this book reflect common, though often unspoken, concerns for many men. We hope you will find reading this book more than a passive endeavor. The chapters have been structured to allow you to read, to reflect on your own experience, and to consider new ways of defining yourself. Each chapter begins and ends with a story from the life of one of the authors. The story illustrates the theme presented in that chapter. Each chapter also contains consciousness-raising activities and personal development exercises that allow you to respond to the book in a personal way. It is important to try not to rush through the book. You may be particularly affected by an exercise or section; stop and allow yourself to be touched by your own reactions. Reading this book is a journey back to your own experience. Memories that have been denied or devalued may reemerge for examination.

A Note to Instructors and Group Leaders

This book provides a primarily psychological and personal perspective on masculinity. We have intended *Man Alive* to be used as an adjunct to classes about gender roles, men's studies, human sexuality, and the psychology of personal adjustment and to introductory psychology courses. It can also be used as outside reading for men in counseling and psychotherapy or a men's group experience. We believe that the book is an excellent stimulus for journal writing and discussion. In reading this book along with a book on women's issues, both male and female readers might be encouraged to examine similarities and differences in their experiences.

We recommend that the consciousness-raising activities be planned in advance because some of them require access to audiovisual or other materials. The personal development exercises can be used for private journal writing or as a stimulus for discussion. The personal nature of these exercises makes them most suitable to a trusting, confidential classroom or group atmosphere. The references and suggested readings provide resources for further exploration of the themes and topics raised in the chapters.

A Word of Caution

We do not want you to change traditional "male" qualities that you perceive as positive, such as determination, directness, or the ability to reason logically, but rather to consider expanding your repertoire of behavior to allow for a more balanced life. Strength does not preclude vulnerability; intimacy with loved ones does not reflect weakness; and taking care of yourself does not mean you cannot be successful. We expect you to wrestle with definitions of yourself and to resist being classified as a typical male. You may look at your relationships differently and ask those you love for feedback about your behavior and upbringing.

At times, this book may cause you some discomfort and lead you to question your assumptions about certain aspects of your life. At other times, it may prompt you to laugh or cry as you recall events that have molded you into the person you are today. No matter how "together" you feel you are, we expect that you will be challenged and affected in some way by this book.

We can identify with the fear and excitement that comes from a new experience, especially one that involves mucking around inside oneself. Often, the first step toward knowing ourselves better is acknowledging our apprehension as well as our curiosity. We are sure that once you take the plunge, you'll be stimulated by what you find.

ACKNOWLEDGMENTS

We acknowledge our debt to the women in our lives. We have all been freed by the feminist demand for equality and are now poised to move beyond our restrictive, traditional gender roles if we wish to do so. Joining with our sisters, men must now share responsibility for creating a world that affirms both male and female.

We also acknowledge men we have known through our work and our friendships. They have taught us much, and their voices are heard throughout this book. Although you may recognize yourself or someone you know in these pages, be assured that we have changed the names and identities of our sources to ensure confidentiality.

We would like to thank those who reviewed this book and offered many helpful suggestions. These reviewers include John H. Brennecke, Mount San Antonio College; James A. Doyle, Roane State Community College; Edward Lafontaine, Keuka College; Paul Skolnick, California State University at Northridge; Joseph Ventimiglia, Memphis State University; and W. Buryl West, Middle Tennessee State University.

We also want to thank our families and friends for their support in our work. Janet Rabinowitz and Lucy Choisser have created a special place for us to work, write, and play together; without their unselfish support and dedication, this book could not have been written.

Fredric E. Rabinowitz
Sam V. Cochran

CHAPTER 1

WHO AM I?
EVERYMAN IN EVERY MAN

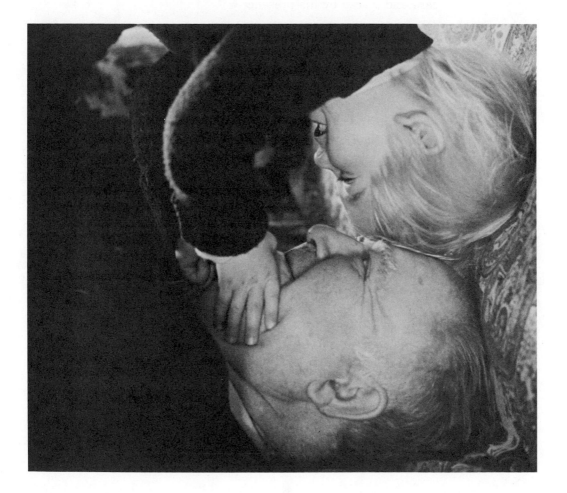

I stood looking at the embalmed body of my grandfather in the wooden casket, lying still with his eyes closed as if he were asleep. I held back my tears despite my memories of our times together. I could recall sitting in the basket of his bicycle as we rode through the city off to visit the fire station or to get bagels for Sunday brunch. Poppy, as I called him, was always looking out for me. As soon as I could balance my bicycle without training wheels I rode behind him, fantasizing that I was protected from the passing cars and trucks by his presence.

He was always telling glamorous stories about his friends and patients from his dental practice. I knew that he had grown up poor in New York City, that he had been a precocious child, and that he had gone on to dental school when he was only 17. I knew that as he looked back at his life he wished he hadn't been so eager to please his own father by becoming the dentist his father wanted him to be. He communicated to me his fantasy of being a psychiatrist, listening and giving advice—as he often did anyway to his patients who lay vulnerable and captive in his dental chair.

Poppy had foibles in his roles of husband and father, but to me he was a wonderful grandfather. I saw how my mother and uncle struggled with periods of anxiety and self-criticism in their efforts to please this man who often expected perfection from himself and his children. Too often he took my grandmother for granted, but in my relationship with him, he was warm, accepting, and encouraging. Maybe he learned as he grew older that he couldn't control the lives around him and that he might as well enjoy the life he had. Maybe I gave him a chance to start over as he guided me, an innocent being, with his love and wisdom. In my last conversation with him, Poppy told me, "The secret to life is to follow your dreams. Do all you want to do, and then you won't have to regret anything at the end. Life goes by quickly."

Even though I felt some hesitation, I was able to cry at my grandfather's funeral. He was one of the few people I knew who accepted me just the way I am. His curiosity about life, his interest in people, and his faith in me, even when I didn't have a sense of myself, sparked me to want to know who I am and to wonder how everyone else got to be who they were. ∎

INTRODUCTION: LOOKING ACROSS THE LIFE SPAN

Life is an epic journey that begins with birth and ends in death. Along the way, developmental milestones mark the path and provide us with opportunities to learn what we need to know to survive as individuals in our family, culture, and species. We come into the world innocent, yet ready to absorb all that we can sense. We seem to be predisposed to grow physically, emotionally, intellectually, and spiritually.

This exciting possibility of an enriched life is constantly challenged by the nature and quality of the learning opportunities passed on to us through our parents and our culture. These powerful influences mold the young boy's vision of his world by selectively rewarding certain thoughts and behaviors and discouraging others. From early childhood through late adulthood, each of us is challenged to make his life meaningful and fulfilling. Often, this process entails struggling with familial and cultural prescriptions and proscriptions that clash with our needs and desires. Both males and females must negotiate a series of passages that confront them with challenges to their identities and sense of direction.

For men, this journey is treacherous. Women outlive men by an average of five to seven years (Nathanson, 1984). Some social scientists suggest that men have a faulty genetic structure (Montagu, 1974), but others stress that traditionally oriented males take more chances with their lives through self-destructive health habits, work in unsafe environments, and deny their vulnerability to forces greater than themselves (Harrison, 1986; O'Donavan, 1988; O'Neil, 1981).

Cultural institutions, as well as the media, have given us a narrow definition of what it means to be a man at various points in our lives. Parents have been socialized to play rougher and touch their infant sons less than their daughters (MacDonald & Parke, 1986). With the exception of such children's shows as "Sesame Street" and "Barney," little boys are bombarded with television programming that portrays masculine characters as tough, strong, aggressive, and in control (Greenberg, 1982; Sternglantz & Serbin, 1974).

Many adolescent males are pressured to conform to a peer group culture that dares them to be aggressive, sexual, and full of bravado (Billy & Udry, 1985; Lueptow, 1984). As young adults, many traditional men rely on a well-paying job, marriage, and a family to give them identity as they drift away from the friendships of the peer group that had been so important to them in youth (Levinson, Darrow, Klein, Levinson, & McKee, 1978). In middle adulthood, many men realize they are dissatisfied with their choices of career, partner, or lifestyle. Some men settle into acceptance of their paths and act as mentors to younger protégés; others change direction (Levinson, et al., 1978). In the twilight stage of life, retirement, the deaths of close friends, and an awareness of being in the final part of the life cycle heightens questions about the meaning of life and challenges each man to come to terms with himself (Erikson, 1980).

Often the stages of life are not as ordered or distinct as has been depicted. Socioeconomic burdens, such as poverty, racism, and lack of opportunities, can significantly change the nature of a man's developmental process. Unexpected crises—such as divorce, trauma, and death—as well as changing jobs, questioning cultural and spiritual upbringing, and making difficult personal choices, also affect the path we traverse. For men of our era, changing gender role expectations and conflicting messages about what it means to be a man leave us challenged to find our way when the traditional signposts fail to provide us with adequate direction.

CHILDHOOD MESSAGES

All children are best served by an upbringing that allows them to trust that their needs will be met by parents or caretakers. A secure base allows the young child to explore his world without fear or impairment (Bowlby, 1988). Despite living in the so-called liberated era, most males are still being raised in ways significantly different from females. Gender identity, the felt sense of maleness or femaleness, is said to be influenced from the moment a parent finds out his or her child's gender (Rubin, Provenzano, & Luria, 1974). Differences in parental interaction styles, expectations of behavior, and even toys given to boys and girls begin the process of gender role socialization. Boys are more likely than girls to be encouraged to play aggressively (Hyde & Linn, 1986), to be physically punished for wrong actions (Hartley, 1974), and to be discouraged by parents as well as by peers from exhibiting behavior that diverges from prescribed gender norms (Fagot, 1978, 1985). Crying and expressing feelings are often kept in check by older males, including many fathers, who remind young boys that "only girls cry." It is not surprising that television fantasy and cartoon heroes convey messages of male heroics through strength, determination, and dominance (Greenberg, 1982). As the boy toddler grows, he is subtly reinforced by his family, peers, and media heroes to equate maleness with toughness, competitiveness, and dominance and to avoid "feminine" qualities, such as dependency, submissiveness, and emotional expressiveness. "No sissy stuff" is the phrase that David and Brannon (1976) coined to describe the avoidance of femininity at all costs.

Psychologists and sociologists who have studied the ways in which our culture promotes differential treatment for little boys and little girls find several explanations for how gender role identity develops in childhood. Social learning theorists suggest that children observe, imitate, and are reinforced by those around them, who often treat them differently depending on whether they are boys or girls (Mischel, 1966). As they learn to speak, little boys and girls begin to categorize themselves. By the time most children are ready for school, they have adopted a gender identity that has consistent and well-defined traits and roles to accompany it, reflected in such phrases as "boys play with trucks" and "girls play with dolls" (Cahill, 1986; Kohlberg, 1966). Psychoanalytic feminist theorists hypothesize that, unlike daughters, who identify with the characteristics of their mothers, sons must learn to cut their empathic ties with their mothers to establish their unique, separate male identity. Little boys, identifying with their fathers, learn to focus on the boundaries between themselves and others rather than on their connections to others. Because many fathers have been raised in a restrictive male culture defined by what they do, they perpetuate the sense of separateness in their sons by maintaining emotional distance and reinforcing independent and autonomous behavior (Chodorow, 1978; Dinnerstein, 1976; Gilligan, 1982). These early experiences provide a keystone of gender-based differences reflected in relationship patterns, values, cognitive processes, moral reasoning, and other domains.

Bill, a man in his early thirties, recalled during a therapy session,

I was around 10 years old and having trouble keeping up with my math in school. I hadn't told anyone how lost I was or how inadequate I felt in the class. I was with my dad in his workshop on a

Saturday afternoon. Even though it was normal for us to remain in silence, I was hoping that he'd put his arm around me and ask me sincerely how I was doing in my life. Instead, he just sent me off to get tools and eventually told me to go out and play since I was distracting him. I felt very hurt and rejected and felt tears forming under my eyelids. I ran outside with my toy machine gun and hid in the bushes behind the house, where I had my secret fort. I remember shooting my gun at birds and pretending that I was a tough army infantryman crawling through enemy territory.

The pre-adolescent boy must make his way through an environment that tells him that his feminine side is to be hidden and that he must show only the tough male exterior if he is to survive as part of his group. Even though he still cries and wishes for a loving parent to take him aside and hug him, he has learned that this part of him makes him unmanly and must be suppressed if he is to emulate his male role models. The fear of being called a "sissy" is so great that many boys take the offensive, punishing those who show their sensitivity and naiveté. Aggressiveness, even in the kindergarten classroom, is more likely to be initiated by boys, with teacher reprimands only reinforcing this behavior through increased attention (Serbin et al., 1973). Sadly, few boys make it through this early stage of their lives with a sense of self that is whole. Instead, we have learned to separate and hide our vulnerability and fears behind a mask of toughness, aggressiveness, and bravado.

ADOLESCENT MESSAGES

Adolescence is a time of physical and psychological change. Although it has been characterized as a troubling and anxious time by many, the way each of us handles this period is unique. Many young men are challenged by the physical and psychological changes that puberty produces, such as the appearance of pubic hair, differing rates of physical growth, and emotional lability. Adolescence is also a time of changing allegiances. The peer group often takes precedence over the family as the basis for establishing one's identity during this period (Berger, 1988; Carter, 1987; Erikson, 1980). Males are more prone to act out conflicts in a rebellious manner through antisocial behavior when they are having trouble fitting into their peer culture or are struggling with divorce, rejection, or chaos at home (Petersen, 1987). Adolescent gangs have proliferated in recent years. These gangs are made up of members who seem to be searching for a common identity in the midst of extreme conflict and lack of structure in their families and communities.

Inside the adolescent male, hormonal changes bring about an acute awareness of sexuality. It is during this time that many males become aware of their sexual orientation. To those whose preference is homosexual, adolescence is often a time of shame and hidden desire. It is not unusual for gay men to look back on these years and recall how different and abnormal they felt. Only in later years, after finding an accepting peer culture, is it possible for them to put their feelings of loneliness and alienation into perspective.

Ted, a 35-year-old gay member of a men's group, remembered the denial of his sexuality during adolescence:

> If only they knew how much I wanted to tell them [his friends] about what I was thinking and feeling. I pretended to go along with the guys, making comments about girls and even dating on occasion. I didn't think anyone would understand me, so I lived in silent desperation, hoping that someday I would become heterosexual or find someone who felt like I did. Fortunately, when I went to college, I joined a gay group on campus and learned that I wasn't alone.

Heterosexuals often experience an atmosphere of heightened competition with male peers for the attention of the fast-maturing adolescent females (Billy & Udry, 1985). Exaggerated locker room boasting and put-downs can lead the young male to feel inadequate about his potency as a man and reinforce a cycle of lying about his feelings and thoughts. Confused about what it means to be a man, many young men try to fit into a narrow, rigid male role that protects them from embarrassment and allows them to be accepted by their peers. During junior high and high school, cliques of "jocks," "partiers," and "car dudes" often seem more attractive than the straight, sensitive, and intellectual types negatively labeled "nerds," "bookworms," and "squares."

Jack, a 16-year-old high school student in the "car dude" clique at a large California high school, reflects a narrow view on life that masks confusion about his role in the world:

> Just give me my [surf]board, the foxiest girl in the school, and a red Porsche with an excellent sound system and I'll live my life in the most radical way. . . . I really don't care what happens when I get older because I'm not going to be like my old man, who works all day and then watches TV until he drops. . . . I want life to be a party.

Compare this statement to that of Frank, a 42-year-old married male in a men's group, who grew up in the same area of California. Frank recalls his teenage years, which he described as conflicted and frightening:

> I was into drag racing and chasing the popular girls. Deep inside I so doubted my masculinity that it was a conscious mission to get their attention, even if it meant getting killed. I also experimented with excessive drinking and had a few secret homosexual encounters with older male friends who I could relate to better than the girls. They [the girls] just seemed like objects to pursue rather than people with depth and feelings. I wish I could go back, knowing what I know now and not caring so much about how I was perceived.

Adolescents struggle to find a way to define themselves. Ethnic and cultural characteristics may become defining factors for inclusion and exclusion from peer groups. It is not unusual to find adolescents experimenting with different cliques during their high school years. Without a clear sense of what it means to be a male adult—except for glimpses of a father who seems tired when he gets home or the celluloid media heroes and antiheroes—the adolescent young man may engage in activities that provide him with a temporary pseudo-identity that is based on fantasy and image. Media depictions of male heroes in the realms of sports, music, adventure, and high finance fuel adolescent fantasies. This dreaming occurs despite the fact that, for example, the chances of becoming a professional athlete are 3 in 100,000 (Leonard & Reyman, 1988). For those who mistake the image of success for reality, activities that provide immediate gratification may take precedence over those that might require discipline and goal attainment. Many other adolescents prematurely foreclose their identities by following a path devoid of experimentation in order to fit in with parental or societal expectations; such men may find themselves experimenting at a later stage in their lives.

YOUNG ADULT MESSAGES

The traditional young adult male has several important tasks in our culture, including choosing an occupation and establishing an intimate relationship that might evolve into marriage, children, and a family (Erikson, 1980; Levinson et al., 1978). Many who choose to go to college often delay entering the adult world. They can explore and experiment with various academic fields, relationships, and work without much of the responsibility of establishing an adult identity. For others, leaving high school begins an era of responsibility for oneself and perhaps for a family. Keen (1991) suggests that a man's first job is his rite of passage into adulthood in our culture. Through work and achievement, young males begin to carve out an adult identity. Making money to buy desired objects, such as cars, clothes, and stereos, allows the young man to feel his power in the adult world. Having been trained since childhood to be goal directed, the young man often has a less conflicted time than his female counterpart in taking on the challenges in the world of work (Bernard, 1981). (Women's conflicts about entering the work force stem partly from the fact that although times are changing, many women have had ambivalent female role models who struggled with decisions about motherhood and career.) Imitating their fathers and grandfathers, young males expect work to satisfy their basic desire to be industrious, important, and productive. When male role models of hard work are lacking, a young man may struggle with what is expected of him in the world of work. It is known in business circles that young men are hungrier for success and thus are often

For many men, establishing a work identity is easier than establishing intimate relationships.

given tough, demanding assignments that older men would rather just supervise. The older men of the culture, who serve as mentors, seem to best teach young men the tricks of the trade. Hidden is the fact that many young men are motivated out of a sense of father hunger, a desire to have a close connection to their father, whose substitute may be found at one's job (Bly, 1990; Merton, 1986). At later points in their careers, many men, experiencing a type of son hunger, rely on their younger protégés to give them a sense of purpose and generativity, as well as to keep their businesses or professions productive when they no longer have the time or interest to continue at the intense pace of their youth (Ochberg, 1988; Osherson, 1986).

Finding a work identity seems to be easier for most men than finding intimacy. Intimate relating, which requires sharing feelings in order to bond, has been a less valued and inadequately learned activity. Few men are exposed to male role models who can show them how to interact intimately with others. Men's communication styles are often oriented toward rational thinking, problem solving, and independent judgment, whereas women's communication is often made up of emotional expression, process statements, and attempts at harmony (Tannen, 1990). The continuing socialization of men not to act "feminine" seems to leave them at a disadvantage in relationships with women. Even so, many men and women get together during their twenties and early thirties and form relationships that result in marriage. It appears that the differences in style and upbringing are tolerated and even valued initially because we have all been raised with male and female ideals that are emulated during mating. It is common for a man to show interest in what a woman is saying and to act romantic and chivalrous in order to win her. Many women, even those who have their own career aspirations, take this courting behavior to be a fulfillment of the fantasy of the fairytale prince sweeping the princess off her feet. Although this mythic interplay of falling in love is repeated throughout our culture, both men and women have difficulty sustaining long-term relationships without developing strong communication skills and a commitment to work out the problems that inevitably arise (Bly, 1990; Goldberg, 1982).

For gay men, young adulthood becomes a time of challenges to authenticity and honesty. Gay young men must make decisions about coming out and establishing intimate relationships with other men. These processes are complicated by the antigay and homophobic sentiments evident in many of our cultural institutions and values. Although many of the basic values of intimacy and interpersonal relationships are common to the heterosexual and homosexual experiences, the challenges to establishing satisfying homosexual relationships are far more substantial (Muchmore & Hanson, 1991).

As prescribed by our culture, many young men become attached to a partner before they have established a sense of complete identity. Some men marry young, have children, and then proceed to spend more time at work than they do nurturing their relationships with their partners and children. The fantasy of future success often clouds the difficult task of balancing an intimate relationship and being a healthy, available parent. It is not surprising that many early marriages result in divorce due to the man's lack of awareness of the problems at home and the woman's sense that she has lost touch with her partner. In the current era, more young men are holding off serious relationships with a permanent partner until they have established themselves in their work arena.

MIDDLE ADULT MESSAGES

With the exception of professional athletes, the middle adult years (35 to 55) are considered the most productive for many men. Work and life experiences combine to produce wisdom in the job setting. Less effort is needed to get the job done, and more time is available to plan and delegate. The provider role allows a man to feel his power at work, but it can distance him from his significant relationships. If he does not make an effort to spend quality time with his partner and children, he may face conflict at home that he is ill equipped to handle. Men who find meaning missing from their work and home life are prime candidates for a period of transition in which they question their life choices. Termed a "midlife crisis," this period may be characterized by a change in career path, divorce, and experimenting with different life-styles (Gould, 1978; Levinson et al., 1978; Vaillant, 1977).

As a man approaches his mid- to late fifties, it is common for him to begin thinking about life after work. Having proved himself in the workplace, he may experience a shift in priorities from achievement and success to a desire to improve the quality of his life. A renewed focus on his relationships with his partner, children, and grandchildren seems to be initiated by his awareness that he has lived more than half of his life. Subconsciously, the thought of his own mortality now makes him consider what is important about being alive (Jaques, 1965). As a younger man, he knew he had to work hard, achieve, be successful, and provide for his family. In contrast, he now looks to his relationships and hobbies as measures of the quality of his life.

Pete, a 52-year-old lawyer, describes the difference in his relationship with his children now and 20 years ago:

I used to work 10 to 12 hours a day, including Saturday and sometimes Sunday. I saw my children when they were getting ready for bed or early in the morning. I didn't have any idea who they were turning out to be, but I was proud that I could provide for them a comfortable, suburban life with a good school. As I look back, I feel like I lost out some on their growing up. Today, I talk with them once a week even though they're grown up and don't need me anymore. I get a high from hearing their voices.

James, a 61-year-old state employee married for 40 years, reflects on his relationship with his wife over the years:

As a very young couple, we were in love and enjoyed each other's company. When we had kids, we focused on them and lost some of the specialness of those early years. After the kids moved out, we went through a crisis. I had been having an affair, and my wife told me that if I didn't go to counseling with her, the marriage was over. I still loved her but had forgotten how to be close. These days, we garden, cook, and take trips together. I'm ashamed that I almost lost this relationship.

On the whole, males seem more interested in understanding themselves in middle age than at any other point in their lives. In middle age, many men renew their appreciation of their partners. Relationships with their children and grandchildren become more important as men realize that the future belongs to their offspring and that they will live on only through their offspring's memories. Middle-aged men recognize life doesn't go on forever and that one cannot control many of life's events.

OLDER ADULT MESSAGES

Stereotypes and myths about the older male abound in our society. Older men are frequently portrayed in the media as incompetent, dependent, helpless, and rigid. Our culture's emphasis on youth often makes men afraid of growing old and facing the last phase of life. Age discrimination is perpetuated by myths. Older men are seen as asexual, rigid, uncreative, incapable of hard work, stodgy, and lacking in intelligence and memory (Levin & Levin, 1980).

Erikson (1980) describes the major life challenge of this period as the development of ego integrity. Many men experience satisfaction when they look back over their lives, especially if they have been productive and successful. Such men have a sense that their lives have been full and have no regrets about reaching the end of the life cycle. For other men, older adulthood brings a sense of dread and despair because life is ending before they have had a chance to feel accomplishment or satisfaction. It is as though they have wasted precious time on work and relationships that were not important. They regret that they did not do what they really wanted to do during their lives.

Lawrence, an 84-year-old retired teacher, reflects on his life:

> It has been a truly amazing experience. I have been fortunate to have had children, grandchildren, and great-grandchildren and the wonderful companionship of my first and second wives. I have been through many crises, but through it all I can say that I always did what I thought was right for us. Sometimes family members and friends disagreed with my decisions, but as I look back I know it all worked out for the best.

In contrast, Ed, a 77-year-old retired accountant, feels resentment about his life:

> I always thought that I should have taken more time to stop and enjoy life. I worked so damned hard to make my family comfortable that I never learned to just enjoy them. Now that my wife has died and my kids rarely visit, I feel cheated. Sure, I have enough money to live on, but I have heart problems that limit my movement, and I'll probably never be able to take that trip to the Far East that I've always dreamed about.

The older man, in his last phase of life, completes his journey. When he reaches the end, he must come to terms with himself and what has been important to him, what he has made of his life. If his journey ends in a hospital room, where he is hooked up to a machine to keep him breathing, he will likely be robbed of understanding the meaning of his life unless he had been conscious of these questions before his final illness. Denial of his own mortality up to this point will likely leave him with little comprehension of how he fits in the larger order of the universe. This is why it is important for the man in older adulthood to reflect on his life, enjoy his relationships, and do what he most values. To look back with few regrets, to appreciate how his teachings will live on through those he has touched, and to grasp the meaning of his mythic journey through life will help the man in the final phase of life gracefully accept his own death.

EPILOGUE

        I still have dreams in which my grandfather speaks to me. As I struggle to lead a meaningful life, his words, "follow your dreams," pierce my waking existence. With so many decisions needing to be made every day, it is easy to become confused about what is important. I know that life is a struggle and that it is important not to avoid the conflicts that are my teachers. So as I traverse this long road of life, I have decided that "following my dreams" will be my beacon. I have to ask myself every day, "Is what I am doing a part of my life dreams?" If it is, then I know it is important, whether it be playing with my daughter or writing a book. I hope to be able to look back at my life and say the same thing to my children and grandchildren: "Follow your dreams. Life goes by quickly."   ■

SUMMARY

This chapter introduces some of the passages and crises facing men throughout their lives. Having been indoctrinated by our culture from an early age to be strong, competitive, and unfeminine, most men have learned to deny important inner signals that allow for closeness with others and self-understanding. It is usually as we grow older that we realize the importance of relationships and the significance of finding meaning in life's journey. By seeing the road signs ahead of you and paying attention to how you respond to life's inevitable challenges, you may be able to navigate the journey with more acceptance, love, and understanding.

CONSCIOUSNESS-RAISING ACTIVITIES
ACTIVITY 1

In dyads (male–male, female–female, or male–female), list five messages about being a man that little boys growing up in our culture are most likely to receive. These messages can come from the father, through male peer groups, from teachers, or from the media.

1. _____

2. _____

3. _____

4. _____

5. _____

List the messages on the blackboard, and discuss them either in small groups, or as a class or group. Tally the number of times a particular message is noted. What does this tell you about the kinds of socialization messages to which little boys are exposed?

ACTIVITY 2

Consider the following incomplete sentence, and generate as many complete sentences as you can using the stimulus. Try to think of as many adjectives as you can with regard to young men and old men.

Young men are _____; old men are _____.

For example, you might say, "Young men are strong; old men are weak," or "Young men are smart; old men are wise." After generating as many sentences as you can, discuss how our culture values old men.

PERSONAL DEVELOPMENT EXERCISES
EXERCISE 1

Think about your role models, and write the names of three of your role models, past or present. After each one listed, indicate what you value about him or her.

1. _____

I value this person because_____

_____

2. _____

I value this person because_____

_____

3. _____

    I value this person because_____

_____

EXERCISE 2

On the following life line place an *X* to indicate each point at which you consider a significant event to have occurred in your life as a male, up to the present time. Review the events you chose. Why did you select these particular events? What meaning do they have for your identity as a male? How have they contributed to the formation of your identity as a male?

_____

Birth   Death

EXERCISE 3

Think back to some of your earliest memories of your father and grandfather. What changes have you noticed in their attitudes, appearances, or behaviors as they have grown older?

    Father: _____

_____

    Grandfather: _____

_____

    How do you feel about these changes? Are there changes you would make in your life now to ensure a feeling of personal integrity late in adulthood?

REFERENCES

BERGER, K. (1988). *The developing person through the life span* (2nd ed.). New York: Worth.

BERNARD, J. (1981). *The female world.* New York: Free Press.

BILLY, J., & UDRY, J. (1985). Patterns of adolescent friendship and effects on sexual behavior. *Social Psychology Quarterly, 48,* 27–41.

BLY, R. (1990). *Iron John: A book about men.* New York: Addison-Wesley.

BOWLBY, J. (1988). *A secure base: Parent-child attachment and healthy human development.* New York: Basic Books.

CAHILL, S. (1986). Language practices and self definition: The case of gender identity acquisition. *The Sociological Quarterly, 27,* 295–311.

CARTER, D. B. (Ed.). (1987). *Current conceptions of sex roles and sex typing: Theory and research.* New York: Praeger.

CHODOROW, N. (1978). *The reproduction of mothering.* Berkeley and Los Angeles: University of California Press.

DAVID, D. S., & BRANNON, R. (Eds.). (1976). *The forty-nine percent majority: The male sex role.* Reading, MA: Addison-Wesley.

DINNERSTEIN, D. (1976). *The mermaid and the minotaur: Sexual arrangements and human malaise.* New York: Harper & Row.

ERIKSON, E. (1980). *Identity and the life cycle.* New York: Norton.

FAGOT, B. (1978). The influence of sex on parental reaction to toddler children. *Child Development, 49,* 459–465.

FAGOT, B. (1985). A cautionary note: Parents' socialization of boys and girls. *Sex Roles, 12,* 471–476.

GILLIGAN, C. (1982). *In a different voice.* Cambridge, MA: Harvard University Press.

GOLDBERG, H. (1982). *The new male-female relationship.* New York: New American Library.

GOULD, R. (1978). *Transformations: Growth and changes in adult life.* New York: Simon & Schuster.

GREENBERG, B. (1982). Television and role socialization: An overview. In National Institute of Mental Health, *Television and behavior: Ten years of scientific progress and implications for the eighties* (pp. 179–190). Washington, DC: U.S. Government Printing Office.

HARRISON, J. (1978). Warning: The male sex role may be hazardous to your health. *Journal of Social Issues, 34,* 65–86.

HARTLEY, R. (1974). Sex-role pressures and the socialization of the male child. In J. Pleck & J. Sawyer (Eds.), *Men and masculinity* (pp. 7–13). Englewood Cliffs, NJ: Prentice-Hall.

HYDE, J., & LINN, M. (1986). *The psychology of gender.* Baltimore, MD: Johns Hopkins University Press.

JAQUES, E. (1965). Death and the mid-life crisis. *International Journal of Psychiatry, 46,* 502–514.

KEEN, S. (1991). *Fire in the belly: On being a man.* New York: Bantam Books.

KOHLBERG, L. (1966). A cognitive-developmental analysis of children's sex-role concepts and attitudes. In E. Maccoby (Ed.), *The development of sex differences* (pp. 82–173). Palo Alto, CA: Stanford University Press.

LEONARD, W. M., & REYMAN, J. M. (1988). The odds of attaining professional athlete status: Redefining the computations. *Sociology of Sports Journal, 5,* 162–169.

Levin, J., & Levin, W. C. (1980). *Ageism: Prejudice and discrimination against the elderly.* Belmont, CA: Wadsworth.

Levinson, D., Darrow, C., Klein, E., Levinson, M., & McKee, B. (1978). *The seasons of a man's life.* New York: Knopf.

Lueptow, L. (1984). *Adolescent sex roles and social change.* New York: Columbia University Press.

MacDonald, K., & Parke, R. (1986). Parental-child physical play: The effects of sex and age of children and parents. *Sex Roles, 15,* 367–378.

Merton, A. (1986). Father hunger. *New Age Journal, 94,* 22–29.

Mischel, W. (1966). A social-learning view of sex differences in behavior. In E. Maccoby (Ed.), *The development of sex differences* (pp. 56–81). Palo Alto, CA: Stanford University Press.

Montagu, A. (1974). *The natural superiority of women.* New York: Collier Books.

Muchmore, W., & Hanson, W. (1991). *Coming out right: A handbook for the gay male.* Boston, MA: Alyson.

Nathanson, C. (1984). Sex differences in mortality. *Annual Review of Sociology, 10,* 191–213.

Ochberg, R. (1988). Life stories and the psychosocial construction of careers. *Journal of Personality, 56,* 173–204.

O'Donovan, D. (1988). Health and femiphobia. *Men's Studies Review, 5*(2), 14–16.

O'Neil, J. M. (1981). Patterns of gender role conflict and strain: Sexism and fear of femininity in men's lives. *The Personnel and Guidance Journal, 60,* 203–210.

Osherson, S. (1986). *Finding our fathers: The unfinished business of manhood.* New York: Free Press.

Petersen, A. (1987, September). Those gangly years. *Psychology Today,* pp. 28–34.

Rubin, J., Provenzano, F., & Luria, Z. (1974). The eye of the beholder: Parents' views on sex of newborns. *American Journal of Orthopsychiatry, 44,* 512–519.

Serbin, L., O'Leary, K., Kent, R., & Tonick, I. (1973). A comparison of teacher responses to the preacademic and problem behavior of boys and girls. *Child Development, 44,* 796–804.

Strenglantz, S., & Serbin, L. (1974). Sex role stereotyping in children's television programs. *Developmental Psychology, 10,* 710–715.

Tannen, D. (1990). *You just don't understand: Women and men in conversation.* New York: Ballantine Books.

Vaillant, G. (1977). *Adaptation to life.* Boston: Little, Brown.

Suggested Readings

Chodorow, N. (1978). *The reproduction of mothering.* Berkeley and Los Angeles: University of California Press.

DOYLE, J. (1989). *The male experience*. Dubuque, IA: William C. Brown.

ERIKSON, E. H. (1980). *Identity and the life cycle*. New York: Norton.

FARRELL, W. (1986). *Why men are the way they are*. New York, NY: McGraw-Hill.

GERZON, M. (1982). *A choice of heroes*. Boston, MA: Houghton Mifflin.

GILLIGAN, C. (1982). *In a different voice*. Cambridge, MA: Harvard University Press.

GOLDBERG, H. (1976). *The hazards of being male*. New York, NY: New American Library.

KEEN, S. (1991). *Fire in the belly: On being a man*. New York: Bantam Books.

LEVINSON, D., DARROW, C., KLEIN, E., LEVINSON, M., & McKEE, B. (1978). *The seasons of a man's life*. New York: Knopf.

MEAD, M. (1975). *Male and female: A study of the sexes in a changing world*. New York: Morrow.

PLECK, J. H. (1981). *The myth of masculinity*. Cambridge, MA: MIT Press.

PLECK, J. H., & SAWYER, J. (Eds.). (1974). *Men and masculinity*. Englewood Cliffs, NJ: Prentice-Hall.

CHAPTER 2

FROM SON TO FATHER

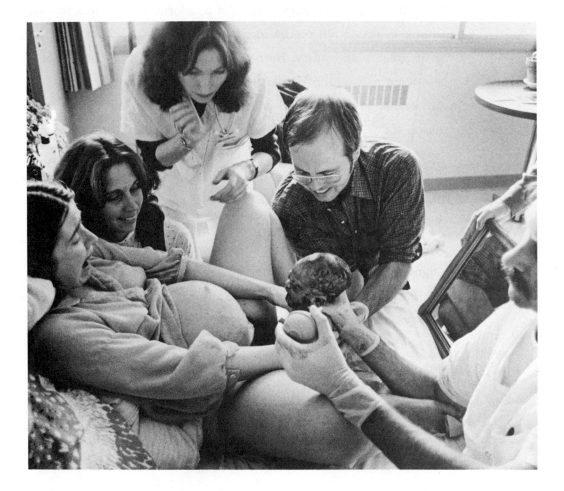

In spite of all our preparations for the impending birth of our child, I was caught off guard when the doctor said to Janet, my wife, "I think you should stay in the hospital tonight. The baby is close. We'll deliver it in the morning." Our bag of clothes, snacks, and survival items was back at our apartment. I looked at Janet, who was hooked up to a fetal monitoring device, and assured her I'd go back and get all we needed.

As I raced to our apartment, a 25-minute walk from the hospital, I came unglued. Images of a deformed baby or a mother dying in childbirth reminded me that delivering a baby was not without risk and worry. Here we were in a foreign country, where we were minimally literate, trusting Janet's life and that of our unborn child to people we barely knew. I had not anticipated this burst of anxiety since I had been calm and confident throughout the pregnancy.

Nervously I gathered up our hospital supplies and headed back into Salzburg, Austria, where we lived. I quickly climbed the steps to the third floor of the hospital to Janet's room. To my horror, she was gone. The bed had been moved but she was nowhere in sight. I frantically ran down the hall looking for a nurse. No one was around. "I can't believe I'm going to miss my child's birth," I thought to myself. I didn't even know where the birthing room was. I went down to the hospital entrance and asked the only person I found where the birthing room was, in English. She looked at me funny. "Oh great," I thought. Then out stumbled a phrase I knew in German, but as quickly as the woman responded, I lost the meaning of what she had said. I told her to take me to the birthing room. As I reached the room, I spotted Janet lying calmly on the special birthing bed with the midwife nearby. "You didn't have the baby, did you?" I blurted out. "No, I just got here a few minutes ago." I breathed a sigh of relief, donned my medical gown, and entered the room.

As the contractions waxed and waned, I stood by Janet and let her tell me what she needed from me. Much of the time, it was just my presence or a touch of hands. I daydreamed, thinking about my father and what he must have experienced waiting for me or my brothers to be born. It dawned on me that back then, fathers didn't usually attend the birth. He was probably out in the waiting room, pacing, smoking a cigarette, or maybe he was at work, waiting for the phone call to tell him when his child had been born. I felt lucky to be living in these times, since I wouldn't want to miss this for the world.

It was time for Janet to start pushing. I stood behind her, supporting her head, as she slowly moved the baby through the birth canal. In what seemed like a short time, the crown of the head appeared and then out came the baby, attached by the umbilical cord, kicking and crying. It was a girl, and she looked wonderful. After the cord was cut, she lay on Janet's chest. I was relieved. After taking some pictures, I held my baby daughter, Karina. It is hard to describe in words the joy and love I was feeling. ■

INTRODUCTION: THE LEGACY OF FATHERS AND SONS

Since we enter life dependent on our parents or caretakers for nurturance, support, love, and physical sustenance, they influence our development in powerful ways. It is common for boys to feel emotionally closer to their mothers and to have mixed feelings about their relationships with their fathers (Wright & Keple, 1981). Probably one of the most difficult tasks for a son is separating from his mother and identifying with his father as he grows into a man (Chodorow, 1978; Greenson, 1966). Because his mother represents warmth, comfort, and closeness, a young man feels a great loss when he enters the world of his father, which is more separate and lonely. Our culture does not give men a chance to grieve this loss, which results in strained relationships between men and between men and women (Bly, 1990). Men must come to terms with their relationships with each of their parents in order to become healthy adults and parents (Bradshaw, 1988; 1990). From a gender role perspective, men must unlearn the distancing behavior of their fathers in order to become more involved in their relationships, especially with their own children. It is only recently that many men have begun to transcend the modeling they received and to be active and invested partners and fathers. Along with their involvement as parents, however, has come increased anxiousness about the children, traditionally a part of the mother's domain (Kort & Friedland, 1986). While there is still some discrepancy between what men say they would like to do and what they actually do in child care, the gap seems to be closing. This is especially true since more women have entered the work force (Pleck, 1985). Society has been slow to accept men's increased involvement, especially for nontraditional fathers who do not fit the white, middle-class stereotype.

THE SON'S SEPARATION JOURNEY TO MANHOOD

The triangular relationship the son has with his mother and father has been written about throughout the ages (Campbell, 1949). In the Greek myth of Oedipus, the son who has been sent away early in his life returns unknowingly to his family of origin, killing his father and marrying his mother before he realizes who they are. In the Grimm brothers' fairy tale, "Iron John," a young man leaves his family of origin with the help of a wild man to seek his destiny. Before he leaves he must steal the key to the wild man's cage from under his mother's pillow (Bly, 1990). In Homer's *Odyssey,* Telemakhos struggles with the absence of his father, Odysseus, as his mother is besieged by male suitors. To resolve his conflicted feelings and establish his identity as a man, he must go out and search for his lost father (Fitzgerald, 1963). These stories symbolically depict the son's passage into adulthood, one in which he must separate from his mother, grieve his lost connectedness, and join the world of men by seeking out and getting to know his father. When this process is interrupted, the young man is often left with unresolved feelings that prevent him from fully embracing his manhood.

Freud (1917) postulated that early in the first few years of life, the little boy so enjoys the loving relationship he has with his mother that he wants her all to himself and fantasizes disposing of his father so this can occur. In Freud's interpretation, the father remains and unconsciously threatens the young boy with castration, teaching his son to give up his exclusive love of his mother and to identify with the masculine strength of his father. Chodorow (1978) took this concept a step further by suggesting that it is not the threat of castration but rather a socialization process that is taking place. In order for the little boy to become a man, he must renounce his close connection to his mother and begin to emulate his father, who lives in a world of separateness and boundaries. Imitating his father, media influences, and cultural institutions all help to socialize the young boy into the male role (Brannon, 1976). The young boy feels terror and abandonment as he leaves the attachment to his mother. In our culture, many boys learn to devalue their female side, which seeks closeness, comfort, and softness, as a defense against the longing they feel from this separation (Osherson, 1986). A fear of vulnerability, engulfment, and dependency is often carried into adulthood in the form of a pseudo-independence that leaves men tough on the outside but empty and sad on the inside (Keen, 1991). A man's unspoken grief of losing the bond with his mother occasionally finds expression in the presence of a woman who can be trusted. The longer this grief is held in, however, the more likely it is to come out in an extreme form as either clinginess or rage, rather than a deep sharing of sadness. This can be frightening for a woman who is trying to have an equal and mature relationship with the man (Osherson, 1986).

Until recently men did not speak to each other about their grief and pain. They could not go to their fathers with their pain because many fathers were not emotionally equipped to help their sons understand and accept such feelings. The fathers were also in denial (Bly, 1990). The average man accepted the notion that he would try to get his need for contact and comfort from the woman in his life, who would come as close as she possibly could to emulating his lost mother. The rest of the time he would lead his life alone and separate from his fellow men. With the exception of team work and competition, he would not risk intimacy with other men for fear of showing his vulnerability. Occasionally, a man might share his pain while he was intoxicated, with the excuse of his drunkenness to negate the emotional intensity of his message.

Until a man learns to grieve the loss of the warmth and nurturance of his mother, he will have ambivalent feelings about his relationships with women. On one hand, he will put women on pedestals as his emotional saviors, while at the same time he will devalue them for the power he has given them to fix his never-healing wound (Osherson, 1986). The distance from his father must be bridged for the son to know what it means to be a man. Otherwise superficial appearances will be all a boy knows about his father. The son will never know the thoughts, feelings, and struggles of the father, and he will have no guide for how to share himself with his children when he is a father (Bly, 1990).

THE SON'S SEARCH FOR HIS FATHER

The decade of the 1980s saw an explosive acknowledgement of the importance of fathers' roles in the psychological and spiritual development of their sons. Several authors highlighted the previously unrecognized importance of the fathers' emotional presence in their sons' lives (Blos, 1985; Corneau, 1991; Osherson, 1986; Pleck, 1987). While not all father-son relationships are troubled, many seem to be affected by the historical and cultural roles that have molded men. Beginning in the industrial revolution, when fathers left their homes to work in factories, the father's daily absence from the home resulted in the loss of a realistic model of how to be a man. Once fathers became breadwinners who went off to work all day, sons caught only glimpses of their fathers rather than getting to know their full presence. Instead of being inspired and encouraged by his father, the young man received only the residue of his tired mood after a long day at work (Bly, 1990). The result of this gulf between father and son has been articulated in three basic themes: the absent father, the lost son, and peacemaking with the absent father.

LONELINESS: THE LEGACY OF THE ABSENT FATHER

A father can be absent in a number of ways. He can be physically absent due to death, separation, divorce, or other forms of direct absence from the family. The father can also be absent by overvaluing the importance of working, of being the breadwinner. He might spend many hours at his job, rising to catch the train or bus to the office before the rest of the family is awake. He might come home late, sometimes after dinner has already been served and cleared from the table. He might work late hours, missing much of the social and interpersonal interaction that often occurs in the evenings in traditional families. A father's absence can also be emotional. The father can be so rigidly encased in his role as breadwinner that he is unable to function effectively as a caretaker. He may avoid emotional contact with his son, maintaining distance. He might discourage horseplay, physical play, and other forms of traditional father-son interaction that often builds more intimate relatedness. Emotional absence can also be due to substance abuse, depression, extremes of mood, anxiety, and a host of other internal factors that frequently create insurmountable barriers to intimacy (Friel & Friel, 1988).

The absent father impacts his son in a profound way. As the growing boy ventures out of his orbit around the mother, he begins to seek out a connection with his father. This natural growth process is compromised when the father is consistently absent and unavailable to the son. An emptiness or longing may be felt in this situation that becomes the foundation on which a deep sense of loneliness develops. A man who is lonely at his core never learns to experience himself in relation with other men, and consequently may have great difficulty developing and maintaining male friendships later in his life (Osherson, 1986).

The son who experiences this father-absence or father hunger, as it has been called by recent theorists, may express it later in his life as a longing for closeness with an older man, someone who can show him the meaning of manhood, who can initiate him into adulthood (Bly, 1990). He may seek mentors, spiritual advisors, or therapists. He may attempt connection with strong women, thinking the emptiness will be filled by a transformative relationship. However he chooses to express this longing, a man will ultimately be compelled to recognize its source, a lack of connection on a deep and fundamental level with his father. Only through taking a close look at himself and his feelings, and then at his relationship with his father, will a man be able to find a way out of his dilemma.

THE LOST SON: SEEKING CONNECTION

From an early age, the son whose father is absent behaves in ways that are unconscious attempts to connect with his father. A boy's misbehavior in the home, on the playground, and in the neighborhood are examples of early attempts to involve a man in his life. Little boys who express their longing in these ways frequently are expressing a need for limits to be set on their behavior. The wish is for an understanding, firm, yet nurturing father to step in and restore an equilibrium that is missing in their lives. If this need continues unfulfilled, misbehavior at school or in the home often becomes more exaggerated. Fighting, acting out in the classroom, and other forms of negative, attention-seeking behavior may ensue.

As the growing boy enters junior high and high school, opportunities for being lost multiply. The young man may continue in the vein of misbehavior and develop a life-style of delinquency and opposition to forms of perceived authority. The longing may be deeply internalized and result in depression, alienation, or substance abuse. Another form the longing may take is perpetual mediocrity and ineffectualness, in which the young man never manages to attain his potential academically, occupationally, or interpersonally. Lack of direction, career confusion, perpetual indecision, and the resulting unhappiness are mostly reflections of an absence of the father that has now been so deeply internalized that the young man's every action reflects an attempt at reconnection.

CONNECTING WITH THE ABSENT FATHER

Frequently, through these experiences of failure, loss of self-esteem, and frustration, the young man will recognize a need to modify many elements of his life-style. He will seek ways to make new choices, pursue new opportunities. Often, a young man's ability to pursue such rewarding life changes effectively is connected with his recognition of his deep sense of loss and pain in response to his emptiness and lack of adequately developed inner strength. Inner strength is built from qualities, traits, habits, and values learned through direct experience with the father.

Although deeply painful, the acknowledgment of his father's absence and the impact it has had leads the way to a man's growth. The man now has a deep understanding of the source of much unhappiness and frustration in his life. He also has a number of venues by which to repair himself. Many support groups, therapy groups, workshops, books, and other resources are available to support the man in these efforts. A consistent theme in this work is the recognition of the need for reconciliation with the absent father. This is a grieving process in which the loss is finally acknowledged after a period of denial, then strongly felt, and finally accepted. When the opportunity to re-create the relationship with his father arises, it can lead to a profound transformation for both the man and his father. When the opportunity for reconciliation is non-existent, a final mourning for the lost father must be pursued. A true acceptance of his relationship with his father can lead a man to feel a sense of freedom and empowerment that has, up to that point, been unattainable.

Trevor, a 45-year-old member of a men's therapy group, lamented:

> My father was a strong man, but he never let me close to him. He worked a lot of the time I was a little boy growing up. I idealized him even though I didn't know him very well. He was always well dressed and running off to important meetings. When he asked me how I was doing, I would always tell him "great" even if it wasn't true. I wanted him to care about me, and I accepted any crumb he threw me. Now, I mostly just feel sad about our relationship. There was so much unspoken emotion between us that I wish we could

have talked about and shared, but we never did. Now that he is gone, I wish I could have told him I loved him.

THE FATHER OF THE NINETIES: A NEW ROLE

In spite of the temptation to rely on the father roles passed down through family and culture, each man must contend with his own unique set of circumstances, opportunities, and limitations. This uniqueness makes the decision to become a father a very personal and individual event, one that cannot be forced into the molds or boundaries of a particularly defined role or set of roles. Although most decisions a man makes are reversible, at least in theory, becoming a father is not one of them. When a man becomes a father, he assumes responsibility for another person. He must be prepared to selflessly offer himself—his material, emotional, and spiritual sustenance—to his son or daughter for many years to come. It is a decision not to be taken lightly. It is a complex, difficult, and challenging decision fraught with ambivalence and anxiety for most men.

A man may have a number of motivations for becoming a father. Perhaps one of a man's most compelling reasons for choosing fatherhood is the desire to extend his family lineage. How a man feels about himself and his own family is reflected in his desire to keep his name alive in future generations. Another important reason for becoming a father is a desire to transmit to his children the cherished values he has struggled to discover within himself. The desire to provide for one's children that which was not provided for him is a deep and compelling need in every man. A desire to share in the parenting of a son or daughter with a loved one is another strong motivating force for choosing fatherhood. The quietly emerging awareness of a desire to complete one's developmental tasks is yet another reason why many men choose to become fathers. They may feel they will miss out on an important experience if they forego fatherhood. For men who want a family and are unable to conceive, the dream of being a father may lead to frustration, anger, and doubts about their masculinity. It is usually necessary for men to work through these emotions before considering adoption as an alternative to natural fathering (Osherson, 1986).

The decision to become a father inevitably engages a man in looking back at the experience of growing up in his own family and in looking forward to his dreams, fears, and hopes about the father he will become. He begins to scrutinize his relationship with his own father on a very personal and emotional level. "What was my father like as a man?" "In what ways am I like him?" "What values did he transmit to me as I grew up?" "What values do I want to transmit to my children as they grow up?" "How does becoming a father affect my view of myself as a man?" These are some of the many questions a man asks himself as he thinks about becoming a father. On this personal, emotional level there are as many different roles and experiences of fatherhood as there are men who are fathers.

EXPERIENCING FATHERHOOD

Our fathers and their fathers had limited roles in the planning and preparation for parenthood. Their roles were typically restricted to carrying on with the day's work, providing whatever emotional support that could be mustered for the wife and her condition, and then taking his obligatory place in the hospital waiting room and pacing, smoking cigarettes, and nervously awaiting news of the delivery. Child rearing was typically seen as the woman's responsibility. The man's job was to carry on with the work, bring home the paycheck, and administer discipline when necessary. Researchers in the late sixties and early seventies found that fathers who were tradition-

Many fathers harbor a strong desire to provide physical and emotional support for their children.

al breadwinners spent less than 10 minutes a day of quality time with their infants (Pedersen & Robson, 1969; Rebelsky & Hanks, 1971). In more recent studies of dual-career couples, it has been shown that as more women enter the work force, more men are spending a higher percentage of their time with their children (Jump & Haas, 1987; Pleck, 1985).

Today there are many more options for the father-to-be to consider. Men may choose to attend their partner's prenatal health care visits. They may take an active part in educating themselves about pregnancy and the vast changes that are occuring in their partner's body. Childbirth preparation classes such as Lamaze have mushroomed in popularity as a reflection of this greater involvement by fathers. Courses are even being taught on preparing for the practical and psychological aspects of fatherhood (Levant, 1990). Over a 10-year period from 1974 to 1984, the percentage of fathers attending the births of their children rose from 27% to 80% (Lewis & Sussman, 1986) and is probably even higher today.

The expectant father may choose to take on additional roles around the house, helping out wherever possible as his partner experiences a new sense of exhaustion and physical evolution unknown to her, especially if it is her first pregnancy. A man may choose to anticipate many of the difficult questions about child rearing and participate actively in an open dialogue with his partner about the ways he will take part in the care of his daughter or son. Previous generations of men might have ignored, or been unaware of, many of the day-to-day, moment-to-moment details of childrearing. Who will get up in the middle of the night and change the baby's diapers? Who will stay home with the newborn? Who will mix the formula? Will child care be used, and if so, what qualities will be sought in a child care setting? The most important factor in dealing with the myriad questions and issues that will certainly arise is open communication between the man and his partner. He must be as clear as he can be about his own values and beliefs on certain issues, and he must communicate with his partner about how they wish to handle the child-rearing tasks as a team. Successful and rewarding parenting involves teamwork and open communication, and being a father is being half of the team.

CHALLENGES OF FATHERHOOD

Only recently has the transition to fatherhood been viewed as an opportunity and a challenge, not as a risk or a crisis (Bronstein & Cowan, 1988). This shift in conceptualization of the fathering experience most likely mirrors the positive changes that have been occurring. The father's role in the family has evolved; it is now seen as an integral and positive role in which to be invested and to take pride (LaRosa, 1989; Levant & Kelly, 1989).

Nonetheless, men worry as they become fathers. Often they feel a heavy burden of responsibility for their families' financial and emotional well-being (Kort & Friedland, 1986). The many new opportunities for fathers create more concerns for them as well. To begin with, many men fear that their wives' pregnancies will not work out, that something will happen that leads to a miscarriage, or that some congenital anomaly will result in an imperfect offspring. It is not uncommon to bond or attach quickly to the developing child and develop a deep concern for her or his well-being. As a way of showing this concern, many men become protective and find a capacity for nurturance within themselves that may have been untapped until this moment in their lives (Gerzon, 1982).

Many men are fearful of the effect the new addition to the family will have on them, their partners, and their relationships with their partners. Men may subconsciously fear being displaced as the primary focus of their partner's attention. They know the freedom and luxury of life without children is going to end and that the child will change the lives of all the family members forever (Osherson, 1986).

Men also become concerned about their ability to manage the demands of fatherhood. They doubt they have the capacity to perform effectively as fathers. Men doubt they will be able to learn the seemingly myriad tasks of taking care of a newborn. A man who has never changed a diaper or given a newborn a bath may feel overwhelmed and tempted to opt for the easier way out by deferring to his partner to take over these chores. Staying engaged in these aspects of parenting on a day-to-day level has been shown to be one of the most difficult challenges for many men. In spite of the movement toward a more equitable division of labor in the home, men still spend less time caretaking than their partners, especially if their partners are not working outside the home (Lamb, 1987; Pleck, 1985).

Fathers continue to worry once their children are born about the children's health and well-being. Will the child develop normally? Will the child thrive and be free from overwhelming physical or mental challenges? The father further wonders whether he will be able to protect his child from hurt, pain, and disappointments in spite of the rational awareness that this is impossible.

An additional concern for many fathers is whether their children will be competent in the necessary life skills to begin to negotiate the environment effectively. Will his son or daughter be respected and have friends? Will he or she be able to learn to crawl, swim, teeter-totter, or ride a tricycle? Will they be able to succeed in pre-school play activities on a social as well as instrumental level? Will the child's efforts in kindergarten, or later school years, be a success?

Perhaps one of the most compelling concerns for fathers is their ability to be competent providers. Even though many of the major components of the breadwinner role have faded, this remains a deeply felt responsibility for many men. They wonder about their ability to provide the things their children want or need, such as food, clothing, and education. They want to be able to offer their children enough toys, enough clothes to wear, and enough opportunities to realize their potential. The father who is unemployed, underemployed, or unhappily employed will experience some difficulty integrating the breadwinner aspect of his identity with other aspects of the father role.

Although there are commonalities in the father role, individual circumstances make it virtually impossible to generalize about fatherhood. Each man's experience will be determined by his own relationship with his father and by his unique fashioning of his own role as a father. Adoptive fathers, stepfathers, single, divorced, gay, and physically challenged fathers each have special issues to deal with in their role as parents that may be different from those of partnered biological fathers (see Barrett & Robinson, 1990; Hanson & Bozett, 1985). Different cultural backgrounds will also influence a man's identity and behavior as a father (Endo, Sue, & Wagner, 1980; Gary, 1981; Lamb, 1987; Mirande, 1985). In addition, community norms will further influence the father's role in the family, especially when he is involved in a nontraditional situation. A father who stays home with his child may find a lack of support among his male peers. A gay father may face social ostracism in many middle-class communities. Such diversities create challenges for the father as well as for his children. Despite the potential obstacles in our culture, nontraditional arrangements can potentially provide affirming roles for persons who might otherwise have felt constrained in the typical patriarchal family system.

Gary, a 36-year-old gay man in a men's group, expressed his opinions on his role as a nontraditional father.

> I live in a communal house where there are six of us, and we all consider each other to be family. We share meals together, celebrate our rituals together, and two of us have children. Everyone is called on to help out with child care. My daughter loves the attention she gets in the house. I just couldn't see myself with a straight job, eight-

to-five routine, having my partner raise my children. It just wouldn't be me.

Gerald, a 37-year-old former record company executive, also in a men's support group, reflected on his life as a "house dad" over the past year.

I have never felt better since Betsy became the full-time breadwinner. I was so burned out in my job that this is a relief, although it took some getting used to. The other parents in the neighborhood who stay home are all women. I have finally been accepted into their culture, but I wish there were more men around to share my experience. If it weren't for the support I feel in my men's group, I'm not sure how I'd have handled it. I know that my father would probably turn over in his grave, but I enjoy the time with my children and being really involved in their lives.

Men will continue to be encouraged by spouses and the new male ethic to become involved in child rearing in all of its variations, especially as women make up a greater percentage of the work force. However, until our culture values fathers' emotional and interpersonal contact with their children, there will be incentives for men to stay distant and remain in the provider-only role. Pleck (1986) recommends that men, like those in Sweden and Norway, be given paternity leave by their places of employment so that they can spend more quality time at home at the beginning of their children's lives. It is also important that men follow through on their desire to be more active fathers by learning the essential elements of active child care. Only by approaching and not avoiding the tasks of raising children will men evolve into involved and sensitive fathers.

EPILOGUE

As my daughter grows bigger and becomes more aware of her surroundings and relationships, I am struck by her natural openness and trust in her world. I have had the opportunity to take time off from work so that I could be here every day with her. I shudder to think about all I would have missed if I had been leaving early in the morning and coming home late from work. The myths of men not being able to nurture or support a baby have been just that.

Karina and I have a special relationship where we play, laugh, and feed each other. I feed her her baby food and bottles and she feeds me her spirit of openness and discovery.   ■

SUMMARY

The son must make his way from attachment to separation in his journey to manhood. Resolving the emotional conflict stirred up by this journey is imperative if he is to become a healthy adult. Despite the less restrictive roles now available for men, the role of father is one for which many men are poorly prepared. Unlearning the distancing behaviors learned from their fathers and practicing increased involvement are challenges for men today. Along with the added involvement comes anxiousness that has traditionally been the mother's province. Although some men have difficulty with the transition to being a father and find the tasks of fatherhood overwhelming, more are experiencing the joy and intimacy of knowing their children. Nontraditional scenarios of single fathers, gay fathers, and physically challenged fathers are becoming more commonplace. These deviations from the traditional father stereotype will become more accepted as fathers' emotional involvement in their childrens' lives is valued by our society. Fatherhood is no longer considered a crisis, but rather an opportunity for learning and growth for men.

CONSCIOUSNESS-RAISING ACTIVITIES
ACTIVITY 1

Get together with three other people. Each of you will play a role—one will be father, one mother, one the son, and one the daughter. Sit around a table and role play a dinner scene. If available, have four other people play alter egos with the purpose of speaking what might be unspoken or implicit in the conversations or interactions. As the son or daughter, you might want to bring up a problem on which you want input from the other members. After you have finished the role play, discuss the interactions. What features of men's and women's gender roles in the family did you notice? What was the communication like between family members? From the son's or daughter's perspective, how did you feel about the father's and mother's responses? Were they involved and caring or distant? Talk about your own families of origin to each other and how you handled these types of interactions.

ACTIVITY 2

Look up the word *father* in a dictionary. You will find at least eight or ten definitions. Write these definitions down on a sheet of paper and use each one as the basis for a discussion on the many ways *father* is defined in our culture and the many meanings of the word. How do these various meanings influence our cultural values and norms? Do you see them as positive or negative meanings?

PERSONAL DEVELOPMENT EXERCISES
EXERCISE 1

Think about your father. You might want to look at a favorite photograph of him. Gather an image of him in your mind and write a description of him. Make it as vivid as you can.

_____

_____

_____

_____

Now reverse the roles. Imagine your father looking at a picture of you and being asked to write a description of how he sees you.

_____

_____

_____

_____

What reactions do you have to these descriptions? Did you find this exercise difficult? Did this exercise evoke any emotions in you?

EXERCISE 2

Many people, as they grow older, notice they are more like one or both of their parents than they sometimes care to admit. Think of how you are like your father. What qualities, mannerisms, values, traits, and the like do you and he share? Write down five of these in the following spaces and indicate whether you see them as assets or liabilities.

Quality or trait shared	Asset or liability
_____	_____
_____	_____
_____	_____
_____	_____

What is your reaction to these lists? Are your similarities mostly assets or liabilities? Do you want to do anything differently? For further exploration, write a brief biography of your father that would be suitable for an obituary to be published in a newspaper. What feelings arise as you read your biography of him? What is missing in your knowledge of him?

EXERCISE 3

Imagine you are a father. If you are a father, just think about what this means to you for a moment. How would you want your children to describe you to their friends if they were asked what their father was like? What qualities would they like about you? How do you want them to see you? How would you like them to remember you after they are grown, or after you die? Write down several of these characteristics in the following spaces.

_____

_____

_____

_____

REFERENCES

BARRETT, R. L., & ROBINSON, B. E. (1990). *Gay fathers*. Lexington, MA: Lexington Books.

BLOS, P. (1985). *Son and father*. New York: Free Press.

BLY, R. (1990). *Iron John: A book about men*. Reading, MA: Addison-Wesley.

BRADSHAW, J. (1988). *Bradshaw on the family*. Deerfield Beach, FL: Health Communications.

BRADSHAW, J. (1990). *Homecoming: Reclaiming and championing your inner child*. New York: Bantam Books.

BRANNON, R. (1976). The male sex role: Our culture's blueprint of manhood, and what it's done for us lately. In D. David & R. Brannon (Eds.), *The forty-nine percent majority: The male sex role* (pp. 1–45). Reading, MA: Addison-Wesley.

BRONSTEIN, P., & COWAN, C. P. (Eds.). (1988). *Fatherhood today: Men's changing role in the family.* New York: Wiley.

CAMPBELL, J. (1949). *The hero with a thousand faces.* Princeton, NJ: Princeton University Press.

CHODOROW, N. (1978). *The reproduction of mothering.* Berkeley and Los Angeles: University of California Press.

CORNEAU, G. (1991). *Absent fathers, lost sons.* Boston: Shambhala.

DOYLE, J. (1989). *The male experience.* Dubuque, IA: William C. Brown.

ENDO, R., SUE, S., & WAGNER, N. (Eds.). (1980). *Asian-Americans: Social and psychological perspectives* (Vol. 2). Palo Alto, CA: Science and Behavior Books.

FITZGERALD, R. (1963). *Homer's The odyssey.* Garden City, NY: Anchor Books.

FREUD, S. (1943). *A general introduction to psychoanalysis.* Garden City, NY: Garden City Publishing.

FRIEL, J., & FRIEL, L. (1988). *Adult children: The secrets of dysfunctional families.* Deerfield Beach, FL: Health Communications.

GARY, L. (Ed.) (1981). *Black men.* Beverly Hills, CA: Sage.

GERZON, M. (1982). *A choice of heroes.* Boston: Houghton Mifflin.

GREENSON, R. R. (1966). Dis-identifying from mother. *International Journal of Psychoanalysis, 49,* 370–374.

HANSON, S., & BOZETT, F. (Eds.) (1985). *Dimensions of fatherhood.* Beverly Hills, CA: Sage.

JUMP, T., & HAAS, L. (1987). Dual career fathers participating in child care. In M. Kimmel (Ed.), *Changing men: New directions in research on men and masculinity* (pp. 98–114). Newbury Park, CA: Sage.

KEEN, S. (1991). *Fire in the belly: On being a man.* New York: Bantam Books.

KORT, C., & FRIEDLAND, R. (Eds.). (1986). *The fathers' book: Shared experiences.* Boston: GK Hall.

LAMB, M. E. (Ed.). (1987). *The father's role: Cross-cultural perspectives.* Hillside, NJ: Erlbaum.

LAMB, M. E. (1987). Introduction: The emergent American father. In M. E. Lamb (Ed.), *The father's role: cross-cultural perspectives.* Hillside, NJ: Lawrence Erlbaum.

LAROSA, R. (1989). Fatherhood and social change. *Men's Studies Review, 6*(2), 1–9.

LEVANT, R. F. (1990). Coping with the new father role. In D. Moore & F. Leafgren (Eds.), *Men in conflict* (pp. 81–94). Alexandria, VA: American Association of Counseling and Development.

LEVANT, R., & KELLY, J. (1989). *Between father and child: How to become the kind of father you want to be*. New York: Penguin Books.

LEWIS, R. A., & SUSSMAN, M. (Eds.). (1986). *Men's changing roles in the family*. New York: Haworth Press.

MIRANDE, A. (1985). *The Chicano experience*. South Bend, IN: University of Notre Dame Press.

OSHERSON, S. (1986). *Finding our fathers*. New York: Free Press.

PEDERSEN, F. A., & ROBSON, K. S. (1969). Father participation in infancy. *American Journal of Orthopsychiatry, 39,* 466–472.

PLECK, J. H. (1985). *Working wives, working husbands*. Newbury Park, CA: Sage.

PLECK, J. H. (1986). Employment and fatherhood: Issues and innovative policies. In M. E. Lamb (Ed.), *The father's role: Applied perspectives* (pp. 385–412). Boston: Little, Brown.

PLECK, J. H. (1987). American fathering in historical perspective. In M. S. Kimmel (Ed.)., *Changing men: New directions in masculinity* (pp. 83–97). Newbury Park, CA: Sage.

REBELSKY, F., & HANKS, C. (1971). Father's verbal interaction with infants in the first three months of life. *Child Development, 42,* 63–68.

WRIGHT, P., & KEPLE, T. (1981). Friends and parents of a sample of high school juniors: An exploratory study of relationship intensity and interpersonal rewards. *Journal of Marriage and the Family, 43,*(3), 559–570.

SUGGESTED READINGS

BARRETT, R. L., & ROBINSON, B. E. (1990). *Gay fathers*. Lexington, MA: Lexington Books.

BLOS, P. (1985). *Son and father*. New York: Free Press.

BLY, R. (1990). *Iron John: A book about men*. Reading, MA: Addison-Wesley.

BOWLBY, J. (1988). *A secure base: Parent-child attachment and healthy human development*. New York, NY: Basic Books.

BRADSHAW, J. (1988). *Bradshaw on the family*. Deerfield Beach, FL: Health Communications.

BRONSTEIN, P., & COWAN, C. P. (Eds.). (1988). *Fatherhood today: Men's changing role in the family*. New York: Wiley.

CORNEAU, G. (1991). *Absent fathers, lost sons*. Boston: Shambhala.

KAFKA, F. (1953). *Letter to his father*. New York: Schocken Books.

KRULL, M. (1986). *Freud and his father*. New York: Norton.

LAMB, M. E. (Ed.). (1981). *The role of the father in child development*. New York: Wiley.

LEVANT, R., & KELLY, J. (1989). *Between father and child: How to become the kind of father you want to be.* New York: Penguin.

OSHERSON, S. (1989). *Finding our fathers.* New York: Free Press.

PEDERSON, A., & O'MARA, P. (Eds.). (1990). *Being a father: Family, work, and self.* Santa Fe, NM: Muir.

PLECK, J. H. (1985). *Working wives, working husbands.* Newbury Park, CA: Sage.

CHAPTER 3

THE HIDDEN WORLD OF EMOTIONS

My father had taken me to the father-son breakfast at our local synagogue. Each boy sat with his father at one of several round tables in a meeting room. As I scanned the crowd, I noticed the similarities in appearance and mannerisms of each father and son. I was also aware that I felt uneasy being honored as a nine-year-old in a ritual I didn't understand.

As we ate bagels and cream cheese at this early morning hour, I turned my attention to the speaker, Clay Dalrimple, a catcher for the Philadelphia Phillies. Since I played catcher for my little league team, I was anxious to meet this real-life hero who I dreamed of one day becoming. In reality, Clay Dalrimple had a lifetime batting average of .200 and was not much of a threat for the Most Valuable Player award, even on the last-place Phillies. I don't remember much of what he said, but he seemed like a boyish grown-up with whom I could relate.

The real excitement came with the raffle drawing where one of us could win a major league baseball autographed by Clay himself. The numbers were called out, and I felt a rush of adrenaline when I realized they were calling my raffle ticket number. My smile and lit-up eyes betrayed my pride in my specialness at that moment.

A moment later, I was upstaged by another son in the room who began crying loudly. Even though his father told him to keep his mouth shut, he still screamed out, "I want the baseball!" Most of the men in the room were embarrassed because this boy was expressing his strong desire for my baseball. My father seemed particularly uncomfortable and looked down at me and the ball I was gripping tightly. As the other boy's whining continued, he said,

"Freddy, give him the ball." "What?" I thought. "Give him *my* ball?" My body tensed and I began to feel tears welling up inside of me. My father was giving me strong eye contact that suggested I do what he said.

In that moment, I sucked in my tears and walked over to the crying boy my age and handed him the ball. He stopped crying, and I felt numb. I walked back to my seat, and I noticed my father smiling. He seemed proud of me for sacrificing my prize to keep the peace and shut down the uncomfortable stillness in the room. I heard other men whisper about my action. My dad put his arm around me and said, "Freddy, I am so proud of you. You did the right thing."

"This was the right thing?" I thought. Yes, I was getting the respect of the all-male crowd with my heroic act of self-sacrifice. I knew from that moment on that I would never whine or cry for anything ever again because I saw how they treated the other boy who did. I heard comments about what a baby he was and how immature he had been. Despite having been rewarded for overriding my emotions, to this day I really wish I hadn't given up that baseball. ∎

INTRODUCTION: MEN AND THEIR EMOTIONS

"How do you feel?" "Why don't you ever tell me how you feel?" "What's wrong? Don't you have any feelings?" Men have been criticized frequently and strongly for not knowing or expressing their feelings. This criticism usually is directed to them by partners who desire more intimacy. And there are probably good reasons for this criticism. Men traditionally have not been taught to know or express their emotions (Balswick, 1988; Farrell, 1974). Men are frequently shut off from their emotional selves in order to survive in a world that demands them to pull away from their families and spend more time out of the home than in the home, working at often boring or oppressive jobs. Taking care of business requires men to be focused, on task, and goal directed, qualities we have all been taught to admire and emulate. Indeed, the typical socialization process to which men are exposed from infancy through adulthood gives short shrift to our emotional lives.

There are, as might be expected, both adaptive benefits as well as negative consequences for this distance from feelings. The adaptive benefits have been framed within the achievement and power realms of functioning (O'Neil, 1981; Sattel, 1976). They are the ability to work hard without being sidetracked by emotions, to remain goal directed, to respond calmly to a crisis, and to do the unpleasant things in life that need to be done. The negative consequences are often hidden, or kept hidden: loneliness, isolation, alienation, and physical illness due to pent-up emotions seeking release (Harrison, 1978). Men must learn to balance their adaptive strengths with a respect for and devotion to their emotions, for their emotions are often the basis for friendships, relationships, and important life decisions they must make (Gaylin, 1992).

EMOTIONS: MESSAGES FROM THE BODY

What are emotions? Simply stated, emotions are contextually defined physiological states (Schacter & Singer, 1962). Our bodies are constantly receiving messages from the outside world directing our central nervous system to react, take action, or ignore the message. Each event that is perceived stimulates nerve cells that in turn send chemical and hormonal messages to various parts of our body and brain. Each of these events usually registers some obvious or subtle change in our body chemistry. For instance, if, while driving, someone pulls recklessly in front of you, you are likely to experience a jolt of adrenaline that makes you more alert, focused, and tense. Your breathing and heart rate will speed up. Your behavioral reactions will be modified by previous learning and the dynamics of the current situation. The action you take may be to swerve out of the way and to curse at the other driver if you are alone in your car. If you were with your mother, you might still swerve out of the way but hold the cursing and just mutter to yourself.

The context of this situation provides us with information we use cognitively to assign a mental label or emotion to our physiological state of arousal. While many females have been socialized to identify and respond to the wide and subtle range of arousal states or emotions, males have been taught to minimize their reactions to arousal (Balswick, 1988). Many men's conscious awareness has been blunted of what a feeling is, except in very general terms. Many men label their experiences in terms of intensity rather than subtlety. Anything not registering past the upper- or lower-level thresholds falls into a dull zone. When asked what he is feeling, it is not uncommon to hear a man say "nothing much" or "blank." "I feel good or I feel bad. If you get in my way, I get mad," states Troy, a 46-year-old restaurant owner. While this simple analysis may work for Troy, it usually doesn't reflect the whole story of our rich emotional life.

AUTHENTICITY: WHY SHOULD I KNOW MY EMOTIONS?

You might be tempted to ask the question "Why should I want to identify and experience all those varied arousal states? I like not having to worry about my emotions." Rogers (1980) believed that with true experiencing of our emotions we feel most authentic, honest, and alive. Emotions intensify and amplify our lives, fueling our actions and thoughts.

Emotional states are a barometer of how our lives are going. If we lose track of our feelings, we lose touch with a critical, important element of our lives. Feelings help us understand how we are responding to events in our environment. Happy and exciting emotional states tell us that what we are doing or the situation we are in is giving us pleasure. Humiliating or sad emotional states tell us that what we are doing or the situation we are in is causing us pain. Knowledge of these diverse feeling states helps us understand our current life situation, which might in turn lead to an action that improves it. Struggling with how to respond to conflicting emotions is part of being fully human (May, 1973). If a man tries to avoid or deny a true emotional state, it is not uncommon for him to them make poor decisions or take inappropriate actions that impact others and himself.

Rick, a 19-year-old college student, recalled that he felt apprehensive about going to Tijuana for the night with his friends when he knew that his car needed repairs and that he had to catch up on his school work.

> We got within 20 miles of the border and the car just died. To top it off, one of my friends got alcohol poisoning and had to be taken to a hospital. By the time we got the car towed and got him out of the hospital, I had missed a big exam and didn't have enough money left to pay for the repairs. I wish I had just listened to my initial feelings about this.

Charlie, a 24-year-old waiter, regrets having had a relationship with a woman he said he knew was trouble from the start.

We weren't clicking, but all my friends had told me how cool and beautiful she was, so I kept going out with her. I felt phoney around her, but if I said what I was really feeling I was afraid I'd hurt her. It got to the point where I was so confused about who I was becoming around her that I took a long trip by myself and realized she wasn't for me. Even though I hurt her some by breaking up, it was a relief not to be lying to her or myself.

Living authentically means paying attention to what your emotions are telling you about reality. You may still choose to override this information, but it is important to consider what these emotions may signify. When you become dishonest with yourself through minimizing or denying important emotions or by consciously lying about feelings you have, life becomes more complicated and confusing. Without intending to, you are more likely to bring pain to yourself and those close to you. By acknowledging your emotions, you will find that you are better able to be honest in relationships and to choose friendships, work environments, and play situations that best fit your true personality.

WHY MEN DON'T EXPRESS THEIR EMOTIONS: THE DYNAMICS OF DENIAL

Expressing emotions is probably the hardest task a man undertakes in our culture. Because of our masculine upbringing, we often dismiss our emotions as irrational and useless, something women have that makes them overly sensitive and vulnerable. Passed down by our fathers and their fathers, the taboo on emotions other than anger has often been taught to us early in our lives (Fasteau, 1974). As part of the cultural myth that men must be strong and tough, the vulnerability of emotions like sadness, pain, confusion, or hurt makes us seem weak, defenseless, and dependent. Many a father has told his son, "Quit whining. It's not going to help you get anything done." By denying the range and depth of his own feelings, the father has made it clear to his son that expressing feelings is unmanly and useless. The son learns quickly that the open expression of emotions is dangerous in the world of other men (Bly, 1990). The nonexpression of emotions creates the illusion that we are not really out of control or vulnerable (O'Neil, 1981). If I don't acknowledge an emotion, then I don't have to worry about appearing weak, stupid, or indecisive. In many Asian cultures a man is expected not to upset the family's functioning by expressing disruptive emotions. Displaying emotions not socially sanctioned may bring dishonor and shame to the family.

This powerfully reinforces the prohibition on spontaneous emotional expression in many Asian men (Sue & Sue, 1993).

Even men who want to express their emotions are handicapped by never having been taught a vocabulary for describing their arousal states. It's not that the emotions don't occur, but that we have learned not to tell anyone what we are experiencing (Farrell, 1974). Eventually, our own privacy eludes even us. Many males have gotten so used to not saying anything about their emotions that they no longer even have a way to interpret and label body signals except when they are acute. An ulcer, the flu, a twisted knee get our attention, but a flash of astonishment, curiosity, fear, or surprise only dimly register in our conscious awareness.

Denial or refusal to acknowledge arousal states has been indicted in physical health and psychological problems for men, especially those working under stressful conditions (Sutkin & Good, 1987). Type A behavior, characterized by an aggressive need to achieve and control at the expense of close relationships and emotional awareness, has been a major predisposing factor in heart attacks and chronic illness (Friedman & Rosenman, 1974). The traditional male role that encourages stoicism and working out problems on one's own rather than asking for help seems to have resulted in men's underutilizing medical and mental health services (Good, Dell, & Mintz, 1989; Robertson & Fitzgerald, 1992). Good and Mintz (1990) found that men who adhered to traditional male gender role norms showed higher levels of depression and less use of counseling services than those who were more flexible in their gender role style. Men are three times more likely than women to succeed in committing suicide and many of those who have killed themselves have not consulted with a counselor or therapist before making their life-ending decision (Shneidman, 1985).

The private emotional world of a man is often full of contradictions (Fine, 1988). Many men have experienced a great deal of hidden confusion in their lives as they have tried to live up to expected gender roles and deny the softer, more feminine parts of themselves (Kaufman, 1992). Many men are ashamed to acknowledge or even discuss inner emotional conflict (Osherson & Krugman, 1990). Not knowing or being able to express our emotions has made us less sensitive to the emotions of others. In what Farrell (1974) calls emotional incompetency, many men seem to experience extreme discomfort in the presence of individuals who are fully expressing emotions. Not only does this situation arouse forgotten or unlabeled emotional states within the man, but it hampers his ability to respond genuinely. Lack of empathy and restricted ability to communicate have led many men to become emotionally insulated from others and withdrawn from their

Despite society's unspoken prohibitions, expressing emotion can be gratifying for men.

own inner lives, feeding the stereotype of men as unfeeling and un-expressive.

Sensitivity to the sense of danger men feel in disclosing personal information, especially the emotional component, is needed by those who want to reach the inner man (Osherson, 1992). If a man does not feel safe, he is more likely to withdraw through silence or intellectualization, or to become angry for being pushed to disclose. For men, anger has been a more accepted emotion than many others since it is a common response to frustration as well as a strong defense against feeling shame (Kaufman, 1992).

TYPOLOGY OF EMOTIONS

Cross-cultural studies have demonstrated that most people, regardless of culture, show similar types of emotional expression. Tompkins (1962, 1963, 1987) proposed that humans have eight distinct categories of emotion. Although classified separately, the emotions often overlap, influence each other, and vary in intensity.

The *interest-excitement* emotional state, characterized by dilated pupils, tracking eyes, and an alertness of the senses, reflects the openness of a person to his environment. Curiosity, intrigue, and anticipation are words that have been used to describe this feeling, which is often experienced as pleasurable. Repeated exposure to a familiar stimulus can dull this emotion and lead to habituation. A man needs to find new ways to sense the world, to find some adventure or take time out to change his routine to keep himself curious and interested in his life (Keen, 1991).

The emotion of *joy-ecstacy*, demonstrated by a smile, dilated pupils, and a softness in the facial features, seems to describe the sense of pleasure a person feels when being stimulated or positively reinforced. Joy can be experienced when a desire is being fulfilled, when one is being creative, or a goal has been reached. Often joy is experienced in the moment as the body and mind are free of worry, and there is a strong sense of being fully alive and awake. A man needs to learn what gives him joy and pleasure and reward himself in order to feel positive about life (Lowen, 1990).

The *surprise-startle* emotion, characterized by eye blinks, arched eyebrows, shallow breathing, clenched forehead, and a stiffening body, is one that often catches us off guard. When we are otherwise engaged, an unexpected intrusion of strong intensity may freeze our actions and cause our muscles to strain. Men who put themselves into dangerous situations in their work or are exposed to unexpected stressors often become tense and guarded in anticipation of the unexpected. Because this emotion arises when we are not fully in control, many men work hard to create predictable and controlled routines to keep surprises at a minimum (O'Neil, 1981).

Distress-anguish, demonstrated by tears, arched eyebrows, rhythmic sobbing, and a down-turned mouth, is an emotion that men have learned to avoid as much as possible. Usually in reaction to loss, trauma, or defeat, the experience of emotional hurt and emptiness through crying is a means of psychological release. In our culture, showing distress or grief is a sign of weakness that must be avoided if one is to be a real man. Men feel pain but have few safe outlets to show this emotion. It has been theorized that unexpressed grief is a common experience for men, leading to defensiveness and a numbing of all feeling states (Osherson, 1986).

The emotion of *fear-terror* can be recognized by eyes being frozen open, pale skin, cold extremities, sweat, facial trembling, muscle tightness, and erect hair. Fear occurs when we are confronted with a situation that intimidates and overwhelms us. Often there is a sense of imminent death that is pervasive and leaves one fearing for his life. This emotion is often experienced during war or other potentially violent situations. Soldiers are trained to overcome this fear, even to enjoy it, and not to be afraid to die

(Gerzon, 1982). Even as children, boys are taught not to show fear so they won't appear vulnerable. Some men get hooked on challenging death through dangerous sports or activities in order to experience the adrenaline rush that comes with conquering intense fear. In an extreme form, a man who shows no fear can be dangerous to himself and others by taking unnecessary risks.

Shame-humiliation, characterized by the eyes and head postured downward and a tight mouth and jaw, is an emotional state that results from having one's behavior or a perceived deficit exposed to others and the self (Izard, 1977). Shaming can occur when a parent or significant other disapproves of a child's action or expressed feeling in a way that makes him feel embarrassed and stupid. The child then sees himself through the eyes of the disapproving parent, and over time he eventually loses his own sense of self. The adult who has been humiliated as a child often will be extra-sensitive to interpersonal slights and be apt to humiliate others who show vulnerability (Kaufman, 1992). Many males in our culture have been shamed in some form into giving up their more feminine characteristics and adopting a strong and tough posture in the world (Scher, 1981).

The emotion of *contempt-disgust* can be demonstrated by a sneer, upper lip raised, nostrils flared, and eyebrows down. It is the emotion of aversion, physical as well as psychological. Likely originating as a body defense against poison and noxious substances, contempt-disgust also expresses a desire to repulse and aggressively keep another person at a distance (Tompkins, 1987). It is common for people to experience this defensive emotion when they have been betrayed or severely humiliated.

Anger-rage, distinguished by a frown, clenched jaw, reddened face, intense visual gaze, and muscle tightness, is an emotional state that expresses a man's frustration with himself or another. Often anger overrides other emotional states that may be blocked in a man. It is more acceptable in our culture for a man to experience his rage than his sadness, pain, or shame (Miedzian, 1991). A man whose anger escalates into violence has a problem that must be addressed through legal and mental health interventions.

Any of these feeling states may have been discouraged by parents or peers through criticism of the individual when he was showing an emotion. Imagine a situation where a young boy is confronted by the neighborhood bully who humiliates and scares him. The boy begins to cry and runs home to his father, who tells him to stop crying and be a man. "Men don't cry and aren't afraid. You should have shown him you weren't afraid and fought him if you had to," he says. The young boy's true feelings have been invalidated. The distress-anguish and fear-terror responses were not acknowledged as valid feeling states. Instead, the boy feels shame-humiliation, which he must keep inside since it is also an unacceptable feeling to show. He is reinforced for the contempt-disgust and anger-rage reactions when his father tells him to be tough and fight. The boy has learned the lesson that he should push down his feelings of fear and show only contempt and anger, if anything at all.

In another instance, even joy might be punished in a family where this emotion is seen as silly or stupid. The same little boy might have been happily playing house with a little girl, using Barbie dolls as props. His older brother sees him playing and calls him a sissy for playing with a girl. The young boy's emotional state changes quickly from enjoyment to startle to shame and humiliation. Over time, the boy learns that any outward expression of joy, especially when engaged in "feminine" behavior, might mean shame and humiliation, so he begins to keep his feelings to himself. Because of this shaming, experiencing any emotion becomes dangerous, especially around other men.

Men who abuse alcohol and drugs may do so to break out of the restrictive shell they experience. By introducing a substance that alters consciousness, one can often create temporary emotional states in the interest-excitement and joy-ecstacy ranges. Unfortunately, when the drugs wear off there is frequently a deeper return to numbness or one of the distress-anguish or contempt-disgust emotions. The vicious cycle of creating artificial emotional states and then escaping from them takes the individual farther from, rather than closer to, his own naturally occurring emotional states (Peele & Brodsky, 1975).

ANGER AND AGGRESSION

UNHEALTHY EXPRESSIONS OF ANGER

Male displays of anger and aggression have been sanctioned in many ways by our culture. Many of our movies and television shows depict violence in the forms of threat, rape, and killing. Even sports such as ice hockey and football reflect situations where aggression is needed to win a game (Goldstein, 1983). It is important to distinguish instrumental from hostile aggression (Doyle, 1989). Instrumental aggression, which is acting aggressively to get a job done (for example, pushing aside protestors so a group of minority children can be admitted into a majority school), can be distinguished from hostile aggression, which is aggression intended to hurt people (for example, a car full of gang members with machine guns trying to kill their rivals by spraying fire into another car). It is thought that anger helps to fuel hostile aggression.

Historically, physical aggression and intimidation has been one of the more primitive ways men have shown dominance over each other as well as over women and children (Raven, 1965). Even the threat of violence is a powerful form of control that some men rely on to get their way. Many males have learned in their families of origin and in their peer groups that outbursts of anger are intimidating and frightening. A man can create fear, shame, bewilderment, and sometimes retaliation from those affected by his display of anger. As though compelled, many men repeat this pattern of intimidation even when they want to stop. Jacob, a 23-year-old married man who is a member of an anger management group, described his experience of rage.

> It's like I get so mad that I can't stand the sight of anyone. I've hit my wife, and at that moment, I don't care. Later I can't believe I did it. I remember my father hitting my mother when he was drunk. It used to get me so angry that I wanted to kill him. I realize that I've got to stop because I don't want my son to learn this from me.

Other men have learned that anger itself is an unacceptable emotion. Rather than having direct access to this strong emotion, many men experience a numbness or depression when faced with blocks in their life pathways (Seligman, 1975). Ronald, a 28-year-old architect in individual counseling, revealed, "I never learned how to express anger. My parents forbade it in our house. Now, I seem to back off and avoid confrontation at all costs. Recently, my wife left me, saying that I didn't have enough backbone. I actually agree with her." The result of not expressing anger as it occurs can be an accumulating resentment that expresses itself as a negative attitude toward others, a pessimistic outlook on life, and an inability to feel warm emotions (Shneidman, 1976). Freud (1929) suggested that unexpressed anger turns itself inward causing depression and suicidal ideation.

HEALTHY EXPRESSIONS OF ANGER

Anger that is a spontaneous emotional expression is different from physical aggression or threat. In the former, a person reacts to a situation viscerally, while in the latter there is a manipulative and dysfunctional element, although it may not be fully conscious. Anger is a lower-level response to threat or humiliation originating in the mammalian limbic system that was adaptive for survival (Isaacson, 1982). While anger can still be aroused by frustrating circumstances, there are means of releasing it besides striking out at others violently.

It is important that men find healthy outlets for their anger. The healthy expression of this strong emotion can lead to growth provided that it doesn't come at the expense of hurting or intimidating others (Tavris, 1989). There are two major identifiable components to an anger response. One is physical and the other psychological. The physical aspect of anger is characterized by the strong feeling of body tension that craves some type of release. The psychological element involves understanding the circumstances and causes for one's current emotional state and eventually deciding how to best resolve the situation. If the feeling is so strong that you are afraid to be around people for fear of hurting them, then it is important to be able to walk away from others so that you can be alone. Some therapists tell their clients to count to 20 before taking any action in order to bring down the intensity level (Weisinger, 1985).

Once alone, a physical release can be encouraged by screaming loudly without censoring your words or noises. If you cannot find a sound-proof place, then try screaming into a pillow or sitting in your car and screaming (don't drive the car when you are this angry or you could be putting yourself and others in danger). Some men have installed punching bags to beat on in their basements or garages to allow for a more aggressive physical release. If the anger is part of re-emerging memories of abuse, it is best to find a counselor or therapist who specializes in working with victims of violence and abuse to help you work through these feelings.

When the intense physical edge is off the anger, artistic expression in the forms of drawing, painting, sculpting, writing, dancing, or playing music can serve as a means of making the release a creative and growth-producing experience. As preventative medicine, many men have found that participating in physical sports such as swimming, bicycling, or running reduces everyday body tension and diminishes the intensity of angry outbursts when they occur (Cooper, 1989). For specific physical exercises for tension release, refer to Lowen and Lowen (1977).

Once the aggressive or destructive urges have diminished, it is important to try to understand the origins of your feelings and what you can do about them. If it was the actions of a loved one or friend, it may be necessary to express your feelings in words by saying, "I am really angry at you because you didn't listen to me," or "I'm angry because I feel like you ignored me in front of your friends." Often being able to say words like these allows you to let go of some of the anger and engage in an open and honest conversation about what happened. Often the conversation will go beyond the incident and help both of you understand patterns of behavior that might have led to the outburst. Because many men have not had much experience with this approach, some feel anxious or unsure of themselves when first trying a direct verbal encounter.

If the person toward whom you are feeling anger is not communicative or is unable to respond to your expression of anger in a healthy way, then finding other outlets might be more appropriate. Discussing the situation with a trusted friend or talking with a counselor may help you gain some perspective on the situation and find alternative means of dealing with the anger.

Anger directed toward institutions or faceless authorities may best be channeled through letter writing, grassroots organizing, or nonviolent protest. Joining a group that supports changing unfair practices or discrimination can be a healthy outlet for one's emotional passion.

Greg, a 29-year-old social worker, joined a men's rights group after becoming frustrated with the legal system's bias toward awarding custody of children to the mother regardless of the father's resources and emotional involvement.

> I was so mad at the court for giving my children to my ex-wife despite the fact that I cared for them every day while my wife ran off with her boyfriend. I love those kids and honestly feel they'd be better off with me. I'm still going to fight in court, but I've also found a place within the National Organization of Men to protest on a national level for other men like me who have been discriminated against in child custody suits. Our goal is to change the laws and make them fairer for everyone.

TENDERNESS AND AFFECTION

DIFFICULTIES WITH TENDERNESS

Even more difficult than anger for many men are the emotional states associated with tenderness and affection. If our culture tells us that anger is an appropriate emotion for men, tenderness is definitely out of bounds except when it leads to sexual conquest (Keen, 1991). Tender, warm feelings seem to be almost exclusively the domain of women in our culture and are viewed by many men as unmanly. Such feelings further expose the male as vulnerable and weak (Brannon, 1976).

Many men have been well trained to hide emotions that express love and tenderness, which often leads to difficulties in their relationships and contributes to their feelings of isolation and loneliness (Lewis, 1978). In a relationship, a man's failure to express affection and tender emotions can lead to his partner's dissatisfaction and unhappiness. Many men are criticized for being unable to express tender or warm emotions, and their partners frequently point this out to them. Often, this inability will lead to the breakup of an intimate relationship. Clyde, a 33-year-old man in a men's group, explains how he experienced his tender emotions.

> I get a feeling, like I want to say "I love you" or just put my arms around my girlfriend. But then, for some reason, I just shut down and I don't do anything. It seems like I am going to give up too much by getting too close. Maybe she'll want more than I have to give. This way I can cover myself. But I wind up feeling guilty about not showing her I care.

Although it has been suggested that touch can facilitate self-disclosure and interpersonal communication between men, male-to-male displays of nonerotic affection seem to be limited (Rabinowitz, 1991). Touch, the physical expression of tenderness, is rarely found between men except for special occasions such as weddings and funerals or as an expression of praise and support during participatory athletic events. Men even tend to touch their sons less than their daughters (Barber & Thomas, 1986). Unlike men in certain Mediterranean, Arabic, and Latin American cultures that routinely allow men to hug or even hold hands to acknowledge friendship, the heterosexual North American man tends to be more homophobic. The fear of appearing feminine inhibits many men from displaying affection with each other (O'Neil, 1981).

In one men's group it took six two-hour meetings of self-revelation by members before one of the men initiated touch. After that, the therapeutic work of the group included physical touching for support when appropriate and ended with physical embraces that allowed the men to show their appreciation for each other (Rabinowitz, 1991).

HEALTHY EXPRESSION OF AFFECTION

As a starting point, many men need to take a few moments to reflect on their affectionate feelings. Who do you care about in this world? Who really matters? Who do you appreciate regardless of gender? By acknowledging who you appreciate and care about, you are taking the first step. Although it might be frightening to imagine telling a friend you care about him much less hugging him, it is important to ask yourself "What is the worst thing that is going to happen to me?" Most men and women appreciate knowing where they stand with you.

It is essential to respect another person's personal space, so it is probably unwise to initiate touch with someone you don't know well. With appropriate timing, such as during a greeting or when you are leaving, a touch along with a statement like "It's so good to see you" or "I really appreciate our friendship" or "I just want you to know that you are important to me" may be quite appropriate. If someone has a problem with your verbal or nonverbal expression, the two of you can talk it over and possibly learn more about each other. Overcoming your fear of appearing vulnerable may allow you to deepen your friendship. Letting those you care about know how you feel about them can deepen trust and improve communication in your relationships.

EPILOGUE

Although I was praised for my ability to delay gratification during the father-son breakfast, I never did lose my sensitivity to strong feelings. I just learned to keep them to myself. As an adult I have made a living listening and encouraging people to express their deepest and strongest emotions, but I still hesitate myself. I see that whining little boy and the nasty comments and say "That could be you." However, I have found that when I don't express what I am feeling, I get "emotionally constipated."

Instead of dealing with my feelings about each event that occurs, I get backed up. Sometimes I don't have the time or energy in the moment to make sense of what I feel. Other times I don't trust that the person I have a feeling toward will understand my reactions. So when I come home at the end of the day, I am a conglomeration of emotion that is often amorphous. I sometimes talk to my partner, Janet, but when I am muddled I feel bad about unloading on her. If I can, I try to take a run or bike ride by myself to give my body a release and let my mind sort out the emotional events of the day. I may then write some of this in my journal so I can be aware of what happened and remember how I can handle the situations better next time. After that, I'm ready to be home and enjoy my time with Janet. ■

SUMMARY

This chapter highlights the difficulty men have experiencing their feelings and also ways that men might reconnect with their own emotional states. Emotions are naturally occurring body reactions to perceived events. Combined with our ability to reason, they allow for an accurate appraisal of how to best make our way in the world. While many men have been discouraged from expressing or even acknowledging certain feeling states for fear of appearing feminine, their denial of emotions can have detrimental physical and psychological effects. The emotions of anger and tenderness have been particularly problematic for many men within relationships. Despite our lack of training in learning to identify and express emotions, it is still possible for most of us to learn to acknowledge and relate our feelings to those we care for and trust.

CONSCIOUSNESS-RAISING ACTIVITIES
ACTIVITY 1

Use a class period or an afternoon to do some field work. In small discussion groups, devise a data collection format to use with this activity. The task is to observe men and women expressing their feelings in natural settings such as a shopping mall, a downtown street corner, or a restaurant. Observe such variables as the frequency, intensity, and kind of emotions expressed. Do men and women appear to be similar or different in their expressiveness? Do men express certain feelings with more frequency? Do women express certain feelings more than men? When the field work activity is finished, discuss the findings in class.

ACTIVITY 2

The following exercise has been designed to allow you to focus on what is happening in various parts of your body right now. It may be read by the classroom instructor or group facilitator. Some quiet instrumental music might accompany this activity. The narrator speaks quietly:

Find a quiet spot, shut your eyes, and sit or lie down peacefully. Take off your shoes and try to get your clothing in a comfortable position so it doesn't pinch you. Become aware of how your clothes feel.

Notice how your mind has already started talking to you and distracting you from tuning in to your body. Become aware of your breathing. Take several deep breaths and notice how your diaphragm rises and falls. Follow the rhythm of your inhalation and exhalation and notice how you are keeping yourself alive with your breath. Observe yourself quietly for several minutes.

Move your awareness to your toes, the bottom of your feet, and your ankles. Notice how they feel. Move them around, tense them, and then release the tension. Your feet hold you up all day and yet we rarely acknowledge this feeling of stability or being in touch with the ground. Move up to the calves and squeeze and relax these muscles. Feel their strength and power. The calves help propel you, providing support and mass as you move around in our world.

Tune in to your knees. Roll your knees around and notice how your leg moves in a circular motion. These joints provide flexibility and connection to the lower parts of your leg. If you have soreness or tenderness, notice the pain and how it might affect your movement in the world. Next feel your thighs and hamstrings. Try to experience the tension in these muscles as well as how they feel when loose and relaxed. These muscles connect the pelvis and your legs, giving you the push you need to get out and challenge the world outside of yourself.

The genital area is next. This area is highly charged. It carries the direct expression of our sexuality. Some men feel shame in acknowledging this part of their body, having been punished for masturbating or told they were too sexually aggressive by their partners. Enjoy your genitals and the incredibly sensitive sensations that pulse from this center of male pleasure. Move your pelvis back and forth and notice the natural rhythm that you feel as you move this part of your body. Also be aware of your anus and allow yourself to open and close the sphincter muscle. Under stress and when holding in emotion, many men keep their sphincter tight. Notice how it feels to relax this muscle.

Move up to your stomach. Notice any gurgling or movements. Often, anxiety is felt in this part of your body. Also become aware of your chest. The rib cage protects your internal organs and is the shield for a frontal attack on your being. Feel how it protects you. Pay attention to your spine and back. The backbone protects the millions of nerve connections that allow your body to communicate with your brain. The lower and upper back often ache when a person is under stress or has little chance for emotional release. Notice if there is any tightness in various parts of your back.

Become aware of your arms. Tighten and loosen the muscles in your upper arms as well as in your forearms. Notice the feeling of strength that comes with the tightening and feeling of flexibility that comes with the loosening. Clench your fists and sense the power stored in this tension and then release, noticing each finger and the feelings in your palms. The dexterity of our hands and fingers has allowed us to manipulate objects and touch others in both a gentle and rough manner.

Finally, move to your head. Notice any tension in your neck and the nodules at the base of your skull. Often tension and pent-up resentment are stored in these areas. Become sensitive to your forehead and the area behind your eyes, and notice how it feels to hold your eyes closed tightly and then more loosely. Move down to your jaw. Tense and relax and be aware of how much feeling is held in these muscles. Many men hold back feelings from coming out of their mouths, almost literally biting their tongues to keep from expressing what might be occurring emotionally.

While in this relaxed state, imagine someone you really care about, such as a partner or family member. Be aware of which parts of your body seem to become stimulated while you are visualizing this person. Switch images so that you allow yourself to notice how your body responds to other people and situations in your life. For instance, you might notice how you feel about certain aspects of school or work. Stay with this imaging process as long as you can. When you have had enough of this, take some time to again notice your breathing and state of consciousness. Enjoy the relaxed state and only open your eyes slowly when you are ready.

For many, this is a powerful exercise that in itself might lead to a release of powerful feelings through various body modalities such as tears in the eyes or rumbling in the stomach. For others, it is a technique that allows them to begin to approach their feelings in a safe and gentle way. Remember that feelings are subtle changes in the body that are labeled by the mind in relation to events that are being perceived by the senses. It is also common for internal thoughts, memories, and images to trigger changes in the body that can be expressed verbally as feelings.

You might want to share your reactions to this exercise. How are you feeling now? What was the most enjoyable part of the exercise for you? What was the most difficult part of the exercise for you? How might you use this exercise to help you be in touch with your feelings more? Discuss with a partner or write your reactions in your journal.

PERSONAL DEVELOPMENT EXERCISES
EXERCISE 1

With a partner, discuss the following stimulus questions.

Try to recall the last time you felt an emotion or strong body sensation. Write down this experience and then describe the experience to your partner. What do you remember about this experience?

_____

_____

_____

What label, if any, did you give to this sensation?

_____

How comfortable were you with sharing this feeling with anyone else? What might you fear would happen if you shared this with a male peer? With a female peer?

EXERCISE 2

This exercise focuses on the experience and expression of anger and tenderness. Respond to the following stimulus questions. These questions can be used individually or in dyads or small groups for discussion.

Think of a situation that evokes anger in you. Describe this situation. Who is in the situation? What are the people doing?

_____

_____

_____

       How do you experience anger in this situation? Do you experience a physiological reaction? A mental reaction? A "blank"?

       How do you express or suppress the anger you feel in this situation?

_____

_____

       Now think of someone toward whom you have warm, tender, affectionate feelings. How do you experience these feelings? Are they physiological? Are they a mental state?

_____

_____

_____

       How do you usually express these feelings to the person who is the object of your affections?

_____

_____

_____

Try to brainstorm other ways you might express your anger and tenderness. You might want to shut your eyes and imagine what it would be like to show these emotions in new ways. Later you might want to practice these with people you care about.

EXERCISE 3

Think for a moment about how feelings were expressed or not expressed in your family of origin. Write how each of the feelings listed below were expressed.

       Anger _____

       Love _____

Sorrow _____

Happiness _____

Tenderness _____

Grief _____

Delight _____

Hate _____

Affection _____

Resentment _____

Sadness _____

Joy _____

Rage _____

Warmth _____

Blue _____

Elation _____

What does this exercise tell you about how you express your own emotions? How do you feel about what you have discovered?

_____

_____

_____

REFERENCES

BALSWICK, J. O. (1988). *The inexpressive male.* Lexington, MA: Lexington Books.

BARBER, B. K., & THOMAS, D. L. (1986). Dimensions of fathers' and mothers' supportive behavior: The case of physical affection. *Journal of Marriage and the Family, 48,* 783–794.

BLY, R. (1990). *Iron John: A book about men.* Reading, MA: Addison-Wesley.

BRANNON, R. (1976). The male sex role: Our culture's blueprint of manhood, and what it's done for us lately. In D. David & R. Brannon (Eds.), *The forty-nine percent majority: The male sex role* (pp. 1–45). Reading, MA: Addison-Wesley.

COOPER, R. K. (1989). *Health and fitness excellence*. Boston: Houghton Mifflin.

DOYLE, J. (1989). *The male experience*. Dubuque, IA: William C. Brown.

FARRELL, W. (1974). *The liberated man*. New York: Random House.

FASTEAU, M. (1974). *The male machine*. New York: McGraw-Hill.

FINE, R. (1988). *Troubled men: The psychology, emotional conflicts, and therapy of men*. San Francisco: Jossey-Bass.

FREUD, S. (1929/1974). Mourning and melancholia. In J. Strachey (Trans.), *Standard edition of the complete works of Sigmund Freud* (Vol. 14). London: Hogarth.

FRIEDMAN, M., & ROSENMAN, R. H. (1974). *Type A behavior and your heart*. Greenwich, CT: Fawcett.

GAYLIN, W. (1992). *The male ego*. New York: Viking.

GERZON, M. (1982). *A choice of heroes*. Boston: Houghton Mifflin.

GOLDSTEIN, J. (1983). *Sports violence*. New York: Springer-Verlag.

GOOD, G., DELL, D. M., & MINTZ, L. B. (1989). Male roles and gender role conflict: Relationships to help-seeking in men. *Journal of Counseling Psychology, 3,* 295–300.

GOOD, G., & MINTZ, L. B. (1990). Gender role conflict and depression in college men: Evidence for compounded risk. *Journal of Counseling and Development, 69,* 17–21.

HARRISON, J. (1978). Warning: The male sex role may be dangerous to your health. *Journal of Social Issues, 34,* 65–86.

ISAACSON, R. L. (1982). *The limbic system*. New York: Plenum.

IZARD, C. (Ed.). (1977). *Human emotions*. New York: Plenum.

KAUFMAN, G. (1992). *Shame. The power of caring* (3rd ed.). Cambridge, MA: Schenkman.

KEEN, S. (1991). *Fire in the belly: On being a man*. New York: Bantam Books.

LEWIS, R. A. (1978). Emotional intimacy among men. *Journal of Social Issues, 34,* 101–121.

LOWEN, A. (1990). *Spirituality and the body: Bioenergetics for grace and harmony*. New York: Macmillan.

LOWEN, A., & LOWEN, L. (1977). *The way to vibrant health*. New York: Harper & Row.

MAY, R. (1973). *Man's search for himself*. New York: Dell.

MIEDZIAN, M. (1991). *Boys will be boys: Breaking the link between masculinity and violence*. New York: Doubleday.

O'NEIL, J. M. (1981). Patterns of gender role conflict and strain: Sexism and fear of femininity in men's lives. *Personnel and Guidance Journal, 60,* 203–210.

OSHERSON, S. (1986). *Finding our fathers*. New York: Fawcett Columbine.

OSHERSON, S. (1992). *Wrestling with love*. New York: Fawcett Columbine.

OSHERSON, S., & KRUGMAN, S. (1990). Men, shame, and psychotherapy. *Psychotherapy, 27,* 327–339.

PEELE, S., & BRODSKY, A. (1975). *Love and addiction*. New York: New American Library.

RABINOWITZ, F. E. (1991). The male to male embrace: Breaking the touch taboo in a men's therapy group. *Journal of Counseling and Development, 69,* 574–576.

RAVEN, B. (1965). Social influence and power. In I. Steiner & M. Fishbein (Eds.), *Current studies in social psychology*. New York: Holt, Rinehart & Winston.

ROBERTSON, J. M., & FITZGERALD, L. F. (1992). Overcoming the masculine mystique: Preferences for alternative forms of assistance among men who avoid counseling. *Journal of Counseling Psychology, 39,* 240–246.

ROGERS, C. R. (1980). *A way of being*. Boston: Houghton Mifflin.

SATTEL, J. W. (1976). The inexpressive male: Tragedy or sexual politics. *Social Problems, 23,* 469–477.

SCHACTER, S., & SINGER, J. E. (1962). Cognitive, social, and physiological determinants of emotional states. *Psychological Review, 69,* 436–444.

SCHER, M. (1981). Men in hiding: A challenge for the counselor. *Personnel and Guidance Journal, 60,* 199–202.

SELIGMAN, M. E. (1975). *Helplessness: On depression, development, and death*. San Francisco: Freeman.

SHNEIDMAN, E. S. (1976). A psychologic theory of suicide. *Psychiatric Annals, 6,* 51–66.

SHNEIDMAN, E. S. (1985). *Definition of suicide*. New York: Wiley.

SUE, D., & SUE, D. W. (1993). Ethnic identity: Cultural factors in the psychological development of Asians in America. In D. R. Atkinson, G. Morten, & D. W. Sue (Eds.). *Counseling American minorities: A cross-cultural perspective* (4th Ed., pp. 199–210). Dubuque, IA: Brown & Benchmark.

SUTKIN, L. C., & GOOD, G. (1987). Therapy with men in health care settings. In M. Scher, M. Stevens, G. Good, & G. A. Eichenfield (Eds.), *Handbook of counseling and psychotherapy with men* (pp. 372–387). Newbury Park, CA: Sage.

TAVRIS, C. (1989). *Anger*. New York: Touchstone Books.

TOMPKINS, S. S. (1962). *Affect, imagery and consciousness, I*. New York: Springer.

TOMPKINS, S. S. (1963). *Affect, imagery and consciousness, II*. New York: Springer.

TOMPKINS, S. S. (1987). Shame. In D. L. Nathanson (Ed.), *The many faces of shame*. New York: Guilford.

WEISINGER, H. D. (1985). *Dr. Weisinger's anger workout book*. Oakland, CA: New Harbinger.

SUGGESTED READINGS

BALSWICK, J. O. (1988). *The inexpressive male*. Lexington, MA: Lexington Books.

FASTEAU, M. (1974). *The male machine*. New York: McGraw-Hill.

FINE, R. (1988). *Troubled men: The psychology, emotional conflicts, and therapy of men*. San Francisco: Jossey-Bass.

IZARD, C. (1971). *The face of emotion*. New York: Appleton-Century-Crofts.

IZARD, C. (Ed.). (1977). *Human emotions*. New York: Plenum.

KAUFMAN, G. (1992). *Shame. The power of caring* (3rd ed.). Cambridge, MA: Schenkman.

NATHANSON, D. L. (Ed.). (1987). *The many faces of shame*. New York: Guilford.

STAUDACHER, C. (1991). *Men and grief*. Oakland, CA: New Harbinger.

TAVRIS, C. (1989). *Anger*. New York: Touchstone Books.

CHAPTER 4

MEN AND RELATIONSHIPS: THE STRUGGLE FOR INTIMACY

PROLOGUE

I often wonder if my experience with my first "true love" is typical of other men's experiences. I was a sophomore in college and had fallen for a woman named Wendy. I had endured a painful and frustrating freshman year. While most of my peers had paired off with women, I was too shy even to approach a woman to ask her out. My luck changed during my second year. Wendy and I were living in the same residence hall and met over dinner one night. We struck up a conversation about the differences between the East, where she was from, and the Midwest, where I was from. I figured nothing more would come of it even though I was quite attracted to her. We began to see more of each other at meals and residence hall functions. Gradually, familiarity gave way to more closeness and intimacy, and after two months we were spending time each day together. Frequently we would study together, go out for ice cream, and end the evening with a session of passionate necking.

Then came Christmas break. I went west; she went east. During the three-week hiatus in our daily contact, I missed her and anticipated our reunion when school started up again. When I returned to the campus, I immediately went to look up Wendy. I found her in her room studying, something I thought odd since classes were not scheduled to start for another two days. She barely looked up as she told me she was busy and would see me later. I left her room with a strange, anxious, sinking feeling. After having run into her every day during the fall semester, I found it disconcerting that we hadn't seen each other at all the next day. She was never around when I went by her room, and even though I anticipated her entrance, she didn't appear at my room either. All of my freshman insecurities were returning. "What's wrong with me?" I asked myself.

The next night we finally connected. I found her in a friend's room and awkwardly intruded on their conversation. Feeling a bit foolish, I asked Wendy when she would be free. She said she didn't know. I asked her if we could get together tomorrow after classes. She said she would probably have to go to the library and study. I finally left, defeated but still wanting to find out what had happened to our relationship. I hung around the lounge waiting for her to make her way back to her room. Finally, she appeared. I quickly approached her before she could avoid me again and asked her "What is going on?" She said what I feared she might say. "I don't want to see you anymore. We are just too different." Speechless, I shrugged and walked away, stunned and hurt. We didn't see each other any more, mainly due to her finesse at evading contact as well as my ambivalence about approaching her. As a result of her rejection, I became depressed and eventually went to see a therapist who helped me repair my damaged self-esteem. Her comment that we were just "too different" lingered for a long time as I was forced to reevaluate how I was going to define myself as a man and a person.

■

INTRODUCTION: THE RISK OF COMMITMENT

Alvy, Woody Allen's character in the movie *Annie Hall,* said about relationships, "In some ways a relationship is like a shark. If it doesn't keep moving forward, it will die." When Alvy finds a woman he can trust who seems like an appropriate partner for a good relationship, he begins to find faults in her, to have second thoughts, and to pull back from deeper commitment. Sensing this, his partner begins self-protective distancing, and the game is afoot. This pattern of shrinking from commitment, seeing his partner pull back, then pursuing only to be frustrated is a familiar one to most men and is lamented in many popular self-help books on male-female relationships (for example, Forward & Torres, 1986; Hite, 1987; Lerner, 1989; Richardson, 1983). Alvy's bewilderment and frustration in his search for the "meaningful relationship" mirrors the feelings of many contemporary men. Men have been criticized for being unemotional, unable to commit to relationships, mistrustful of women, and fearful of intimacy. A stereotype image of men as distant and disconnected has been drawn in counterpoint to the stereotype of women as sensitive, emotionally available, and desiring connection. How have men come to be portrayed as so incapable of intimate relating, and is there any validity to these portrayals?

THE IMPACT OF FEMINISM ON RELATIONSHIPS

Since the 1960s, when the women's movement began to experience broad-based popular support among large numbers of women, many men have been on the defensive with regard to their behavior and attitudes in relationships. Women, coming together in consciousness-raising groups, began to criticize traditional gender roles and the behaviors associated with them (Enns, 1993; Freeman, 1984). For men, this meant becoming the targets of criticism about being quiet, dominant, inexpressive, rational, disconnected, and distant. Women had found within themselves another way of relating with others based on values of equality, compassion, understanding, sharing, and respect. As women began to experience the affirming and growth-promoting impact of relationships based on these values, they began to seriously question their male partners and to demand more of them in their intimate relations. The men were bewildered. Unable to respond substantially to these criticisms, men initially withdrew into quiet brooding or lashed out in reactionary anger. There were no examples available for men to observe. There were no vocal advocates for their position on the matter. Men were more or less left on their own to learn how to respond to the women's movement's critique of their behavior (Farrell, 1974; Pleck, 1975).

Gradually, a few men began to analyze and understand their difficulties in relationships. The men's movement of the early 1970s was a strong impetus for these self-questioning men to find support and encouragement to examine their negative and self-defeating patterns in intimate relationships (Shiffman, 1987). Therapists with a special sensitivity to the struggles men experience in relationships also provided an understanding and opportunities for increased effectiveness in interpersonal relating (Scher, 1979, 1981). During the 1990s, more men have begun to talk about their feelings in a supportive context. By sharing their common experiences and concerns, they are beginning to understand how they have been trained to be in relationships and to challenge these assumptions.

COMMON CRITICISMS OF MEN

Some characteristic issues for men have been identified by those who counsel, research, and write about the male experience. Commonly experienced difficulties have been enumerated. While these difficulties have much in common with the criticisms expressed by the feminists, they have provided men with increased self-awareness and opportunities for growth and effectiveness in interpersonal relationships.

MEN AS INEXPRESSIVE

Men have been characterized as inexpressive (Balswick, 1988). It has been noted that we either avoid expressing ourselves or lack a vocabulary for interpersonal relatedness. Without words to label our feeling states, to make ourselves known to others, we have been unable to fully give and receive emotionally. Mike, a 32-year-old male who entered therapy after his spouse asked for a divorce, expressed this difficulty well. "She would always want to know what I was feeling. I couldn't say. I would just draw a blank, nothing." Many men experience the "blank" that Mike describes. When asked what we are feeling, many of us have no words to connect to our internal emotional state. Even if we are aware of an internal state, it often doesn't get verbalized for fear of ridicule or rejection, a legacy of early gender-role socialization prohibiting little boys from having feelings (Goldberg, 1976; O'Neil, 1982). When many boys grow to men, they find they never have had an opportunity to identify and express their feelings in the context of a close interpersonal relationship with another person and are thus challenged by this lack of experience.

MEN AS DEPENDENT

Men have been seen as independent in their gender role orientation to life, but it is in the realm of close interpersonal relationships that male dependence is often encountered. The pattern of male inexpressiveness and lack of self-disclosure often causes many men to be perceived as passive and overly dependent on their partners, relying too heavily on them to assume responsibility for addressing emotional issues in the relationship (Lerner,

1989; Pleck, 1980). This masculine silence baffles the mate and may make him or her wonder about the status of the relationship. Does he love me? Does he really want to be here? As soon becomes apparent for many men, passivity and avoidance of interpersonal dialogue frequently leads to a breakdown of communication.

MEN AS DOMINEERING

Men are also frequently criticized for being overpowering or dominant in relationships (Doyle, 1989). Little boys are socialized to present themselves in control of their emotions, to stand up to threats and face them, to exert dominance on the playing field, and to avoid appearing vulnerable. This learning often leads men to behave in controlling and domineering ways in their intimate relationships. This tendency may manifest itself in overt controlling behaviors such as a loud voice that overrides the other person, rigid positions on issues between the partners, and debating to win a point or defend a position (Tannen, 1990). At extremes, overt controlling behavior may erupt into physical intimidation and violence when the man feels too threatened or vulnerable (Gelles & Straus, 1988).

Covert strategies are also used by men to control their interpersonal relationships. As mentioned, passivity is a frequent stance men adopt in relationships that often results in the partner feeling controlled or manipulated. Agreeing to a request and then backing out or failing to follow through is another frequently utilized covert strategy to maintain control in a relationship. The ultimate covert controlling strategy is one where the man simply abandons any responsibility for the relationship, leaving his partner wondering what happened.

Don, a 32-year-old insurance salesman, related the experience of dominance in his marriage. "I would get so angry at times I would just start shouting. And I can be pretty intimidating when I am angry. That would usually get her to shut up. Then it is easy to get your way."

MEN AS INSTRUMENTAL

Men are typically socialized to be what is known as *instrumental* (David & Brannon, 1976; O'Neil, 1981). When being taught to be instrumental, we are taught to act and to do as opposed to relate and to take care. In most traditional nuclear families men have been shown that the proper, socially sanctioned role is to work outside the home, to earn an income, and thereby support the family. The traditional partner's role is to tend to the emotional and interpersonal needs of other family members, to work in the home. This division of labor may make for efficiency, but it severely restricts each partner from learning a wider range of ways to behave. The man in this traditional role-bound relationship is frequently left with incomplete or underdeveloped relational skills. He may not know how to take care of the emotional needs of others, or how to be comfortable just relating. This instrumental-expressive juxtaposition is a common theme in many studies of men and their relationship patterns (Balswick, 1988; McGill, 1985).

In studies of how men relate in small groups, a consistent finding is that men position themselves in instrumental roles (Eagly, 1987). These include roles that promote action, seek to accomplish a task, and press for closure and decisions. In spite of being functional in task-oriented or working groups, such behavior frequently is perceived as lacking in sensitivity, understanding, and tact in interpersonal relationships. Others' feelings are often ignored as the man presses to get things done. Ann and Con, a couple in marital therapy, expressed a common theme. Ann said, "I don't want you to try to solve my problem. I just want you to listen." Con retorted, "But what is the point of talking if you're not going to do something about it?" This is a classic example of the instrumental male voice.

MEN AS SEPARATE AND INDEPENDENT

Upon further examination of the male approach in relationships, a number of social scientists have observed that the instrumental-expressive dichotomy may be a result of the male's earliest experiences in relatedness (Chodorow, 1978; Gilligan, 1982; Osherson, 1986). In being born to and taken care of by a woman in our culture, a little boy learns first to experience himself in relation to someone unlike himself. As he must later develop his own sense of continuity and connectedness with those like himself, he must break the bond with the mother and seek other bonds with men. This typically occurs with the father. To establish his gender identity, the little boy must bolster his sense of difference and separateness in his first relationship. He must firm up his boundaries between himself and his mother in order to know himself as a little boy and, later, as a man. In so doing, he often sacrifices the sense of relatedness he experienced with his mother. He moves away from her toward an independent identity but still has residual longings for this relationship. A common pattern for the man is to strive to overcome his feelings of loss and abandonment by acting strong and independent and to avoid getting too close to others.

It is not difficult to infer the problems this might cause in later attempts at interpersonal intimacy. Men often complain of being threatened as they enter a relationship and the partner begins to demand more intimacy, commitment, and involvement (Farrell, 1986). It is this dilemma, to

Boys are taught from an early age to act tough and to discount feelings of weakness and fear.

maintain a firm identity or give it up, that is likely at the heart of many common relationship problems for contemporary men. We have learned from sociological and psychological studies of these patterns that men tend to overvalue their autonomy and independence, often at the expense of relatedness to those most important to them in their lives (Cochran & Peplau, 1985).

MEN FEAR FEMININITY

Recently a number of writers have observed that men are deeply fearful and conflicted about appearing feminine (for example, Gaylin, 1992; O'Neil, 1981). Through socialization, little boys are taught from an early age to devalue and discount the feminine aspects of others, themselves, and our culture. Western values, patriarchical family and social structures, and competitive academic and economic systems all promote masculine traits such as independence, toughness, authority, and denial of fear, and discredit feminine traits such as connectedness, sensitivity, understanding, and emotional expression. Many boys learn to devalue their feminine side as a defense against the longing they feel from their original separation from their mothers (Osherson, 1986). When boys internalize an antifeminine value system and become fearful and avoidant of anything feminine in themselves, they learn to be restrictive emotionally, to be dominant in relationships, to be frightened by homosexuality, and to overvalue power, competitiveness, and independence (Brannon, 1976; Fasteau, 1974). Because of its rigidity as a value system, the fear of femininity can lead to relational difficulties with others as well as internal conflict around self-definition (O'Neil, 1990). In later years, as a result of the denial of their feminine aspects, many men find themselves increasingly isolated and disconnected, unable to tap into the nurturant, supportive, and understanding aspects of themselves that have been buried (Jung, 1953; Moore & Gillette, 1990). John, a 29-year-old graduate student in therapy over a series of broken relationships, revealed, "I finally realized that basically, in order for me to be intimate with Joyce, I had to be what I felt was wimpy, gay, a homosexual. I know it's pure craziness. We had great sex, and I always felt like a man with her. But deep down I just didn't want to feel so feminine."

MEN AND WOMEN IN RELATIONSHIPS

THE ROMANTIC MYTH

Throughout history stories about true love and romance have flourished despite the fact that most marriages before the 17th century were not based on love (Doyle, 1989). One version of the romantic myth that appears in popular books and movies such as *Camelot* and *The Princess Bride* involves the appearance of the strong and virile white knight who arrives to rescue the beautiful maiden. They fall in love and ride off into the sunset. The chivalrous male of the Middle Ages has been characterized as strong and loyal, a devoted partner who would do anything for his lady's honor (Doyle, 1989). This romantic fantasy is still alive in our present era, guiding the behaviors and expectations of many young men and women.

Despite our beliefs about practicality and realism in relationships, there is still an attraction within our Western culture to the notion of falling in love. Both men and women have idealized expectations of their potential mates that very few of us can live up to. For men, it is the image of a young, beautiful, and virginal woman. For women, it is the image of a strong, handsome, and successful man who makes everyone else seem not quite good enough. In reality, most of us settle for someone who does not meet these high standards. However, it is not uncommon for the initial stage of an intimate relationship to reenact the romantic fantasy. The infatuation phase, as it has been labeled, is a stage in which each partner is invested in getting to know the other and presenting himself or herself to the other person as an attractive and desirable partner. In this phase of the relationship, negative qualities of the other are often minimized or denied and positive qualities of the other are often idealized. Each partner seems to see in the other that which they have been missing or wanting. It is difficult to sustain a long-term relationship based purely in fantasy. This is why difficulties in relationships seem to occur when the initial infatuation begins to wane (Lerner, 1989).

FRIENDSHIP: TRUST, HONESTY, AND CLEAR BOUNDARIES

Platonic friendship between males and females used to be distinguishable from romantic relationships by the presence or absence of sexual attraction or fantasies about a future relationship. In today's world, men and women have relationships based on common interests and a desire for companionship as well as on physical attraction that may or may not lead to a romantic relationship. The most important issues in a male-female friendship are trust, honest communication, and clear boundaries (Reid & Fine, 1992). Both men and women need to feel that what they share is kept private and not a piece of gossip to be passed along to others. It is imperative that both persons be truthful with each other. While it has been typically difficult for men to share their feelings, it is much easier for them to do so when they feel confident that what they say won't be used against them or that their vulnerability will be exploited. The maintenance of clear boundaries helps to clarify where the relationship stands so that signals are not misinterpreted.

Men have more recently been accused of violating personal boundaries, especially in cases of date or acquaintance rape (Koss, Leonard, Beezley, & Oros, 1985). While men more likely to commit date rape are characterized by their beliefs in traditional gender role stereotypes, beliefs that women should not put themselves in unsafe situations, and a linking of coercion to sexuality, it is still difficult for a woman to know a man's intentions when out on a casual date. To counteract the violation of boundaries, it is important that each of the parties make their intentions clear. If you are comfortable only with a friendship, say so. Too many times ambiguous personal boundaries have led friends to take their relationship to a physical level with unexpected results. If the desire to make a friendship into a physically intimate relationship is mutual, then the relationship may change into a more intimate one for both people. If one person is uncomfortable with a change like this, then it is important to speak directly about it. For either partner, it is better to say "no" or "I enjoy the relationship the way we have it" than to engage in a sexual relationship that is not mutual.

COMMUNICATING WITH EACH OTHER

Tannen (1990) describes how men and women's conversational styles differ. Women tend to use language that encourages rapport, connection, and a desire to understand what a person is saying. Men seem to be better at telling stories, making points, and displaying knowledge. Joking also distinguishes the genders. Many men seem to be more comfortable than women making fun of others and use this mode to communicate with each other. It is not uncommon for men who know each other well to use profanity or sexual references to identify each other. Men also can show insensitivity to the feelings of others when joking in the presence of those not in their "in group" (Lyman, 1987). Abusive or insulting speech may be perceived by others as demeaning and may diminish the speaker's credibility.

Stereotypical styles of relating are learned behaviors that at times make communication difficult between the sexes. If men and women are to communicate, they must practice understanding each other's meaning, not just the words used. Knee-jerk reactions of outrage must be tempered with an attempt to understand the context of what a person is saying. Indiscriminant joking or storytelling must be tempered by the awareness of the possible impact a joke or story has on those present. You can learn to listen for the feelings and not just the facts and it is desirable to do so if you are to engage in any type of relationship, whether it be with a friend, colleague, or intimate partner.

Egan (1976) presents an excellent introduction to communication skills. Attending to another person with eye contact, adopting an open stance, and paying attention to him as he speaks are good ways to begin the process of listening. Nonverbal cues also send a great deal of information. Check the combined information you receive from nonverbal and verbal communication with the speaker. "Do I understand you to be saying . . . ?" "What I hear you saying is. . . ." If your interpretation is confirmed, the conversation can continue. If you are wrong, the speaker can clarify what he or she is saying. As the speaker, it is important to be clear about what you are trying to communicate to the listener. Using a lot of words, not giving the other person a chance to respond, or using impersonal language are ways to muddle your message and miscommunicate. It is best to use the word "I" when expressing a personal feeling, thought, or belief. For instance, it is clearer when you say, "I feel uncomfortable talking with you right now because I have a class I'm supposed to be at" than to say, "Don't you have a class you're supposed to be at?"

While much has been written about communication and the skills involved, it is most important to practice. If you are single and want to improve these skills, it is recommended that you speak with a counselor who can refer you to an interpersonal growth group or attend a workshop in which these principles are practiced. If you are in a relationship, then visiting a counselor or therapist or attending a couple's workshop might help you work on some of these skills.

MEN AND MEN

MALE FRIENDSHIP

Researchers have found that men and women tend to have the same number of same-sex friendships (Caldwell & Peplau, 1982; Fischer & Oliker, 1983). What differs is what occurs within these same-sex relationships. While women were more likely to share feelings and discuss a wide range of personal and relational topics, men were more likely to talk about activities, work, or hobbies and to avoid personal and relational topics (Brehm, 1985; Davidson & Duberman, 1982; Farrell, 1986). Men have also been observed to be less self-disclosing about personal information to other men than to women (Fox, Gibbs, & Auerbach, 1985). What makes men less personally disclosing and cautious in their same-sex relationships?

One hypothesis is that men use less personal self-disclosure in order not to appear vulnerable. Taught to view each other as competitors in the world by the male socialization process, they feel that disclosing personal information is like giving ammunition to the enemy (Derlega & Berg, 1987; Lewis, 1978; Seidler, 1992). The fear many men internalize about being perceived as feminine also works against the development of intimacy between men (O'Neil, 1981). Men in North American culture are taught from an early age that they must not act like sissies, lest they be mistaken for homosexuals. Talking personally and with emotion exposes a feminine weakness that must be avoided at all costs. This leaves only impersonal topics and joking as acceptable means of same-gender communication.

Many fathers also contribute to the lack of intimacy between men by not speaking personally with their sons (Osherson, 1986). Bly (1990) suggests that married men spend more time maintaining their lawns than their friendships. Research bears him out. Married men were less likely to self-disclose with a same-sex friend than single men (Tschann, 1988). Many men lament the absence of true friendship past the secondary school days. David, a 38-year-old college professor, noted, "I work with a lot of men, but we rarely share what's really going on with each other. I don't really have any other male friends that I can be close with." Joe, another college professor, described his hard-won friendships with his male colleagues.

> I have a group of about six other guys, and we usually plan one outing a year, a camping trip or backpacking trip for about a week. We all prioritize it, and we work hard to make it happen each year. It is truly special, and I wouldn't trade it for anything. It takes work, though. I think men are just not naturally inclined to connect with each other.

Male friendships must be pursued and maintained if they are to deepen beyond acquaintance. Letich (1991) suggests the following steps. First, a man must recognize his desire for a male friend and overcome his homophobic attitudes about wanting this type of connection. Through contact in the community, through a men's group, or even looking up an old high school buddy, identify a man you would like to get to know better. In a nonthreatening way, plan to do an activity together. Take the risk to talk personally about yourself and ask personal questions, but not so quickly that you scare each other off. Finally, arrange for regular contact and talk about how much you value the friendship. While this process may take months or even years, it is well worth the male bond that forms.

All-male support groups and retreats can provide new opportunities for men to explore relationships with one another in a safe and nonthreatening atmosphere, much as women's consciousness-raising groups did for them during the sixties and seventies. Many men express excitement and satisfaction at being able to be more open and revealing to each other. This sharing has allowed many men to involve others, in addition to their partners, in meeting their intimacy needs.

GAY RELATIONSHIPS

Gay men have additional challenges in developing intimacy with one another. In addition to contending with their own internalized homophobia, they must also overcome our culture's tendency to marginalize gay men who are openly homosexual (DeCecco, 1984). In spite of the advances made in the eighties in accepting homosexuality, it is still a risk for a man to come out to family, friends, and associates (Marcuse, 1988). Friendships among gay men seem to be less characterized by the traditional male prohibitions on touching and self-disclosure and·are generally more open and personal (DeCecco, 1988; Nardi, 1992).

For gay men, finding a partner is another challenge, especially in this time of heightened awareness of the HIV virus and a continuing climate of homophobic values in our culture. Nonetheless, once a gay man has found a partner who shares common aspirations, values, and goals, the relationship is likely to endure and develop in the same way heterosexual relationships do (McWhirter & Mattison, 1984; Peplau, 1988). Despite their different sexual orientations, the search for intimacy, a feeling of connection and brotherhood, is a common bond linking gay, straight, and bisexual men.

BEING ALONE: BEFRIENDING YOURSELF

It is not reasonable to be in an intimate, established relationship at all times, nor is it reasonable to expect to always be in pursuit of one. There are times when a man will, by choice or necessity, be alone. Solitude can be very difficult for many men, since we are socialized to define one aspect of our self-worth through how we fantasize others will perceive our partner and what the reflection our choice of partner means for us as men. Some men compulsively seek connection, cruising the bars or health clubs, trying to get a date wherever they can find one. These men are frequently left alone since their compulsive searching inadequately hides their deeper insecurity and anxiety about themselves. These men often are destined to repeat a frustrating and never-ending cycle of illusive searching and disappointment. They are alone, but deeply uncomfortable with their loneliness.

Other men accept their aloneness and use it as an opportunity for self-exploration and growth. Moustakas (1977) suggested that loneliness could be the impetus to spark self-reflection and creativity. It is often said that the experience of losing an intimate relationship teaches us what being a man is really about (Kushner, 1981). The self-confidence and security that comes from truly knowing oneself and being comfortable with one's interests, values, opinions, and feelings is unmistakable and often attractive. The opportunity to choose a relationship, as opposed to the need to attach to someone, is a liberating feeling for many men. Herm, a 33-year-old divorced male, reflects this well. "I used to need a woman around to feel whole. After 2 years of living alone, I have finally learned to be my own best friend. I find it's easier to meet women when I am feeling good about myself and not desperately seeking them out."

CHANGING WHAT WE BRING TO RELATIONSHIPS

For many men, the qualities that interfere with our relationships are brought to our attention through a crisis. A partner typically challenges the male to be more involved, forthcoming, and effective in the relationship. The crisis usually comes to a head when the partner abandons or threatens to leave the relationship. As we have seen, such feedback frequently leaves the male bewildered. Most men in this situation complain of having little awareness that anything was wrong. They are angry, hurt, confused, and now beginning to realize that they need to learn some new skills and change the way they think and act in relationships.

Having experienced the challenges and disappointments involved in negotiating interpersonal relationships, a man may recognize a need to take some personal responsibility for his difficulties. He may consult a therapist at the suggestion of a partner who has found his participation in the relationship lacking. If he is lucky and finds a therapist or counselor who is sensitive to men's issues, he may have an opportunity to work in therapy to improve his capacity to function effectively in a relationship. John, the graduate student, explained further: "I just didn't realize I needed to confront this issue about femininity until Joyce left. I was so hurt, lonely, and depressed that I finally decided something needed to be done. I guess you don't miss your water 'til the well runs dry."

Couple's therapy with one's partner is another means of confronting and changing relationship patterns. A therapist sensitive to both interpersonal communication and the conflicts learned in one's family of origin can help a couple explore how their pattern of communication inhibits intimacy and new ways of relating. If a partner has already decided to leave the relationship, this type of therapy may help with the transition involved in uncoupling.

Another avenue for personal growth available to men who want to improve their relationship skills is a mixed-sex or all-male therapy group. Such a group, when facilitated by sensitive and challenging therapists, gives the members an opportunity to enact their ineffective relationship patterns within the context of the group. Each member can receive feedback on these patterns, and try out new and more satisfying patterns with the others in the group. The advantage of the group approach is that members often have the experience not only of receiving constructive input but of giving help to other group members. Such opportunities allow for the development of self-esteem within the context of an interpersonal relationship with another person in the group.

Ultimately, the goal of men's reflection and self-improvement within relationships is the experience of greater intimacy with those they care about. When asked what they most value in relationships, many men respond that they want to be accepted for who they are, they want to feel understood, they want to be respected and not judged, and they want to feel safe (Keen, 1991). This reflects a desire for intimacy, a closeness that is forged from the union of two individuals to create a living relationship within which each continues to exist as well as to receive the love and support of the other. Intimacy implies the capacity for both partners to be who they are, to be able to express themselves freely within the context of the relationship, and not to have their identity defined solely by the needs of the other person in the relationship.

Two essential qualities for intimacy are found in a number of writings. These are the qualities of self-esteem as an individual and self-esteem in relation to others. Self-esteem as an individual involves feeling good enough as a separate individual to be able to make important decisions, navigate necessary developmental tasks, and know that you are a worthwhile individual regardless of your special circumstances. It is something like the ability to be alone with yourself, to be your own best friend. A person who has sufficient self-esteem as an individual does not need to be with another person. He is capable of being happy with himself, but he may choose to enrich his life through relating with another person (May, 1990).

Self-esteem in relation to others involves being able to express one's needs as well as to respond to the needs of others, to listen and be listened to, respect others, and be vulnerable without resorting to control or domination tactics. It implies an attitude of honor and acceptance of the other person, a genuine liking and valuing of them. It is built on a sense of safety in relation to another person that is learned early in life, in the family of origin. Within this feeling of safety, a man often finds he can express himself openly and freely with his partner, without fearing ridicule or rejection. He can accept differences of feeling, attitude, and thought in his partner as signs of strength and character. He can be accommodating and respectful of his partner's special challenges and foibles, recognizing no person is above another when it comes to human frailties.

EPILOGUE

As I look back to that time in college when I desperately needed my relationship with Wendy, I realize that I had not learned to value who I was without external validation from a woman. The breakup with Wendy started me on a search for identity that was based more on how I related in a variety of settings with different people. I was told by my male friends, who felt I had abandoned them during the Wendy affair, that I so easily let our friendships go. As a busy married man with a child, I have to work extra hard to maintain my outside friendships. I use the church as a source for finding male companionship. I also get involved in professional and community projects that have a social component. Even though my co-author and I met 12 years ago and live 2,000 miles apart, in writing this book together, our phone calls, letters, and visits have been a great way to keep our friendship alive.

■

SUMMARY

Intimate relationships are a struggle for many men because of the sociocultural upbringing that tells us to be in control and invulnerable. Raised to be independent, unexpressive, and fearful of our feminine qualities, men have had difficulty sharing feelings, listening for the underlying emotional meaning in conversation, and resisting being domineering and controlling in interactions. Trust, honest communication, and explicit boundaries must characterize our relationships so we are clear in how we relate and listen to each other. Male-to-male relationships are especially difficult for men because of learned fears of appearing feminine and vulnerable to our fellow men, who we often perceive as competitors. Gay men have special concerns in relationships due to North American cultural homophobic attitudes. It is usually only after a crisis in a close relationship that many men become open to getting help from a therapist or group to improve their relating skills. Accepting loneliness as a part of the human experience can make males more sensitive and appreciative of their relationships. Many men who have worked hard to experience intimacy in relationships express satisfaction and relief in being able to express themselves more fully.

CONSCIOUSNESS-RAISING ACTIVITIES
ACTIVITY 1

If you have a television, watch a popular show that airs in the evening hours when most people watch television. Observe how the male character handles his relationships. How does he interact or relate with the other persons on the show? Here are some questions to consider:

1. Does he attend to the other person? That is, does he look at the other person and focus on him or her? Or is he distracted?
2. Does he paraphrase or summarize the other person's speech? Or does he change the subject or not respond to what was said? Does he go off on irrelevant tangents?
3. Does he talk personally? Does he speak of his feelings?
4. When he speaks, do others listen to him and pay attention?

Having observed how men are portrayed in the popular media, how do you feel about this portrayal? Does it remind you of yourself in any way? Do you think it is accurate? Is it fair?

ACTIVITY 2

Pair up with a partner and take turns responding to the following open-ended sentences. Do not limit yourself to one sentence but rather use each phrase as a way to start talking about yourself. The partner who is listening should show nonverbal support through an open body stance and eye contact. When the partner who is talking is finished responding to each phrase, the listening partner should rephrase what the first partner has said, making sure to use a feeling statement. For example, "You are most happy when you feel free to be yourself with no restrictions."

1. I am happiest when . . . .
2. I hate . . . .
3. My biggest troubles in relationships are . . . .
4. I wish that . . . .
5. My father taught me . . . .
6. When I feel vulnerable . . . .
7. I feel strong when . . . .
8. The last time I cried was . . . .
9. Looking at myself makes me feel . . . .
10. Talking to you . . . .

Discuss with your partner how you felt talking about yourself and how you perceived his or her responses to your self-disclosures.

PERSONAL DEVELOPMENT EXERCISES
EXERCISE 1

Consider your parents' relationship. How would you describe it on the following characteristics? (Circle the word that best describes it.)

> Open or closed.
> Happy or sad.
> Equal or unequal.
> Traditional or nontraditional.
> Emotional or unemotional.
> Easy or difficult.
> Troubled or nurturing.
> Sharing or withholding.

What are the implications of this modeling for you and your current relationships? Is there anything you might want to change in these patterns?

EXERCISE 2

We typically learn how to relate to others from the patterns we observe in our own families growing up. This exercise helps you begin to look at how you were shaped in your relationship patterns by the models you encountered as a little boy. Now think about what your relationship models taught you about how to behave in a relationship. Write down the most important things you were taught about how to relate with others.

1. _____

2. _____

3. _____

4. _____

5. _____

Most people identify values like always be polite, never interrupt others, always speak when spoken to, and the like. How does your list compare to these more traditional messages?

EXERCISE 3

Let's consider some of your values about relationships. To do this, respond to the following open-ended questions.

1. If someone wanted to get to know me they would . . . .
2. The most important thing I want to know about someone when we first meet is . . . .
3. You know you're really clicking when . . . .
4. Early on in a relationship it is important for me to . . . .
5. You know the honeymoon is over when . . . .
6. My bottom line in deciding about commitment to a relationship is . . . .
7. The most important thing to do to maintain a relationship is . . . .
8. You know a relationship is going downhill when . . . .
9. The hardest thing about ending a relationship is . . . .
10. After a relationship ends I usually . . . .

Now let's reflect on what your responses mean. Did this make you think of anything in particular? Did it raise questions for you about how you choose to be in relationships?

_____

_____

_____

REFERENCES

BALSWICK, J. O. (1988). *The inexpressive male*. Lexington, MA: D. C. Heath.

BLY, R. (1990). In B. Moyers & R. Bly. *A gathering of men* [Videotape]. New York: Mystic Fire Video.

BRADSHAW, J. (1990). *Homecoming: Reclaiming and championing your inner child*. New York: Bantam Books.

BRANNON, R. (1976). The male sex role: Our culture's blueprint for manhood, and what it's done for us lately. In D. David & R. Brannon (Eds.), *The forty-nine percent majority: The male sex role* (pp. 1–45). Reading, MA: Addison-Wesley.

BREHM, S. (1985). *Intimate relationships*. New York: Random House.

CALDWELL, M., & PEPLAU, L. (1982). Sex differences in same-sex friendship. *Sex Roles, 8,* 721–732.

CHODOROW, N. (1978). *The reproduction of mothering*. Berkeley and Los Angeles: University of California Press.

COCHRAN, S., & PEPLAU, L. (1985). Value orientation in heterosexual relationships. *Psychology of Women Quarterly, 9,* 477–488.

DAVID, D., & BRANNON, R. (Eds.). (1976). *The forty-nine percent majority*. Reading, MA: Addison-Wesley.

DAVIDSON, L., & DUBERMAN, L. (1982). Friendship: Communication and interactional patterns in same sex dyads. *Sex Roles, 8,* 809–822.

DECECCO, J. (Ed.). (1984). *Homophobia: An overview*. New York: Haworth Press.

DECECCO, J. (Ed.). (1988). *Gay relationships*. New York: Harrington Park Press.

DERLEGA, V., & BERG, J. (Eds.). (1987). *Self-disclosure: Theory, research, and therapy*. New York: Plenum.

DOYLE, J. (1989). *The male experience*. Dubuque, IA: William C. Brown.

EAGLY, A. (1987). *Sex differences in social behavior: A social role interpretation*. Hillsdale, NJ: Erlbaum.

EGAN, G. (1976). *Interpersonal living*. Pacific Grove, CA: Brooks/Cole.

ENNS, C. Z. (1993). Twenty years of feminist counseling and therapy: From naming biases to implementing multifaceted practice. *The counseling psychologist, 21,* 3–87.

FARRELL, M. P. (1986). Friendships between men. *Marriage and Family Review, 9,* 163–197.

FARRELL, W. (1974). *The liberated man*. New York: McGraw-Hill.

FARRELL, W. (1986). *Why men are the way they are*. New York: McGraw-Hill.

FASTEAU, M. (1974). *The male machine*. New York: McGraw-Hill.

FISCHER, C., & OLIKER, S. (1983). A research note on friendship, gender, and the life cycle. *Social Forces, 62,* 124–133.

FORWARD, S., & TORRES, J. (1986). *Men who hate women and the women who love them*. New York: Bantam Books.

FOX, M., GIBBS, M., & AUERBACH, D. (1985). Age and gender dimensions of friendship. *Psychology of Women Quarterly, 9,* 489–501.

FREEMAN, J. (Ed.). (1984). *Women: A feminist perspective*. Palo Alto, CA: Mayfield.

GAYLIN, W. (1992). *The male ego*. New York: Viking.

GELLES, R., & STRAUS, M. (1988). *Intimate violence*. New York: Simon & Schuster.

GILLIGAN, C. (1982). *In a different voice*. Cambridge, MA: Harvard University Press.

GOLDBERG, H. (1976). *The hazards of being male*. New York: New American Library.

HITE, S. (1987). *Women and love: A cultural revolution in progress*. New York: Knopf.

JUNG, C. G. (1953). Animus and anima. *Collected works* (Vol. 7). New York: Pantheon.

KEEN, S. (1991). *Fire in the belly: On being a man*. New York: Bantam Books.

KOSS, M., LEONARD K., BEEZLEY, D., & OROS, C. (1985). Nonstranger sexual aggression: A discriminant analysis of the psychological characteristics of undetected offenders. *Sex Roles, 12,* 981–992.

KUSHNER, H. (1981). *When bad things happen to good people.* New York: Schocken Books.

LERNER, H. G. (1989). *The dance of intimacy.* New York: Harper & Row.

LETICH, L. (1991). Do you know who your friends are? *Utne Reader, 45,* 85–87.

LEWIS, R. (1978). Emotional intimacy among men. *Journal of Social Issues, 34,* 109–121.

LYMAN, P. (1987). The fraternal bond as a joking relationship: A case study of the role of sexist jokes in male group bonding. In M. Kimmel (Ed.), *Changing men: New directions in research on men and masculinity* (pp. 148–163). Newbury Park, CA: Sage.

MARCUSE, E. (1988). *The male couple's guide to living together. What gay men should know about living together and coping in a straight world.* New York: Harper & Row.

MAY, R. (1990). Finding ourselves: Self-esteem, self-disclosure, and self-acceptance. In D. Moore & F. Leafgren (Eds.), *Men in conflict* (pp. 11–22). Alexandria, VA: American Association of Counseling and Development.

MCGILL, M. E. (1985). *The McGill report on male intimacy.* New York: Harper & Row.

MCWHIRTER, D. P., & MATTISON, A. M. (1984). *The male couple: How relationships develop.* Englewood Cliffs, NJ: Prentice-Hall.

MOUSTAKAS, C. (1977). *Turning points.* Englewood Cliffs, NJ: Prentice-Hall.

NARDI, P. M. (1992). Sex, friendship, and gender roles among gay men. In P. M. Nardi (Ed.), *Men's friendships* (pp. 173–185). Newbury Park, CA: Sage.

O'NEIL, J. M. (1981). Patterns of gender role conflict and strain: Sexism and fear of femininity in men's lives. *The Personnel and Guidance Journal, 60,* 203–210.

O'NEIL, J. M. (1982). Gender and sex role conflict and strain in men's lives: Implications for psychiatrists, psychologists, and other human service providers. In K. Solomon & N. Levy (Eds.), *Men in transition: Theory and therapy* (pp. 5–44). New York: Plenum.

O'NEIL, J. M. (1990). Assessing men's gender role conflict. In D. Moore & F. Leafgren (Eds.), *Men in Conflict* (pp. 23–38). Alexandria, VA: American Association of Counseling and Development.

OSHERSON, S. (1986). *Finding our fathers.* New York: Fawcett Columbine.

PEPLAU, L. (1988). Research on homosexual couples: An overview. In J. DeCecco (Ed.), *Gay relationships* (pp. 33–40). New York: Harrington Press.

PLECK, J. H. (1975). Men's responses to changing consciousness of women. In E. L. Zuckerman (Ed.), *Women and men: Roles, attitudes, and power relationships* (pp. 102–112). New York: The Radcliff Club of New York.

PLECK, J. H. (1980). Men's power with women, other men, and society: A Men's movement analysis. In E. Pleck & J. Pleck (Eds.), *The American man* (pp. 417–433). Englewood Cliffs, NJ: Prentice-Hall.

REID, H. M., & FINE, G. A. (1992). Self-disclosure in men's friendships: Variations associated with intimate relations. In P. M. Nardi (Ed.), *Men's friendships* (pp. 132–152). Newbury Park, CA: Sage.

RICHARDSON, G. (1983). *No good men.* New York: Simon & Schuster.

SCHER, M. (1979). On counseling men. *Personnel and Guidance Journal, 57,* 252–254.

SCHER, M. (1981). Counseling males: Introduction. *Personnel and Guidance Journal, 60,* 199–202.

SEIDLER, V. J. (1992). Rejection, vulnerability, and friendship. In P. M. Nardi (Ed.), *Men's friendships* (pp. 15–34). Newbury Park, CA: Sage.

SHIFFMAN, M. (1987). The men's movement: An exploratory empirical investigation. In M. Kimmel (Ed.), *Changing men: New directions in research on men and masculinity* (pp. 295–314). Newbury Park, CA: Sage.

TANNEN, D. (1990). *You just don't understand.* New York: Ballantine Books.

TSCHANN, J. (1988). Self-disclosure in adult friendship: Gender and marital status differences. *Journal of Social and Personal Relationships, 5,* 65.

SUGGESTED READINGS

BREHM, S. (1985). *Intimate relationships.* New York: Random House.

CLARK, D. H. (1987). *The new loving someone gay.* Berkeley, CA: Celestial Arts.

DECECCO, J. (Ed.). (1984). *Homophobia: An overview.* New York: Haworth Press.

DRIGGS, J. H., & FINN, S. E. (1990). *Intimacy between men.* New York: Dutton Books.

FARRELL, W. (1986). *Why men are the way they are.* New York: McGraw-Hill.

ISENSEE, R. (1990). *Love between men: Enhancing intimacy and keeping your relationship alive.* New York: Prentice Hall.

JOUARD, S. (1964). *The transparent self.* Princeton, NJ: Van Nostrand.

LERNER, H. G. (1989). *The dance of intimacy.* New York: Harper & Row.

MARCUSE, E. (1988). *The male couple's guide to living together. What gay men should know about living together and coping in a straight world.* New York: Harper & Row.

McGILL, M. E. (1985). *The McGill report on male intimacy.* New York: Harper & Row.

NARDI, P. M. (1992). *Men's friendships.* Newbury Park, CA: Sage.

RUBIN, L. B. (1983). *Intimate strangers.* New York: Harper & Row.

SCHAEFF, A. W. (1989). *Escape from intimacy.* New York: Harper & Row.

TANNEN, D. (1990). *You just don't understand: Women and men in conversation.* New York: Ballantine Books.

TESSINA, T. G. (1989). *Gay relationships.* Los Angeles, CA: Jeremy P. Tarcher.

CHAPTER 5

SEXUALITY: MYTH AND REALITY

I met Ursula at the social service agency where I was doing volunteer work during my first year of college. She was attractive, assertive, and very much in command of her life. Ursula seemed to be able to say without effort what she was feeling at any moment. This intrigued me since I had so much trouble even knowing what I was feeling. We often worked shifts together answering phones and just talking about life.

After a few months, our discussions became more personal. I had found out that she was in the process of breaking up with her boyfriend. I wasn't dating anyone, since I left my high school girl-friend when I went to college. I found myself flirting, making more eye contact, and even finding ways to brush my hand against hers as we spoke. I couldn't quite figure out whether she was attracted to me or was just being nice because we were sharing time and space together.

One night I had a dream in which we were kissing passionately. I took this as a sign that there must be a real attraction and asked her out the next time we were at work. I was ecstatic when she said yes. Following an intimate dinner at a local cafe, Ursula asked me if I wanted to go back to her apartment. I was very excited and probably would have done anything she asked me.

We sat together on her living room couch and began to kiss and touch each other. After a few moments, Ursula surprised me by saying, "Let's go to the bedroom." Even though I was turned on, it seemed pretty fast to be bolting into the bedroom. I was so enamored of her that I readily agreed, although I still didn't feel quite ready to go all the way with this woman I was just getting to know.

As she pulled off my clothes, I got into the moment and began pulling hers off too. We continued our passionate kissing. Birth control quickly came to my mind but before I could say anything, she blurted out that she was on the pill. In the pre-AIDS era this was enough. We were soon having intercourse. I ejaculated within seconds but kept the rhythmic motion going to please her since she was just starting to get excited. I also feared that she would perceive me as a lousy lover if she knew of my premature ejaculation. When it seemed like a long enough time, I faked a moan and pretended to have an orgasm.

She lit up a cigarette. I didn't smoke. I felt awkward lying in her bed, having just experienced a very intimate sexual act, with nothing really to say. Our relationship changed that night from being good friends to being lovers. For me, some of the magic was gone from our flirtatious encounters. I wished that we had taken longer to get to know each other physically. Later, I realized that I could have spoken up and said, "I'm not ready to make love yet," but as a young 18-year-old man, I did what I thought was expected of me.   ■

INTRODUCTION: DIMENSIONS OF THE MALE SEXUAL EXPERIENCE

It is difficult to describe the average or normal male sexual experience because men understand and respond in a variety of ways to this pleasurable, but psychologically complex, physiological activity. Zilbergeld (1988) wrote an enlightening book, *Male Sexuality*, that outlined many of the myths of sex that both men and women believe are necessary elements of the sexual experience. These myths include the notions that a man cannot show vulnerability, all physical contact must lead to sex, sex should always be natural and spontaneous, a man must always be ready for sexual activity, a man must have a hard penis to enjoy sex, a man must be in control of the sexual experience, intercourse is the only true sexual experience, and the goal of sex is to have an orgasm. Zilbergeld went one step further and asserted that the ultimate myth is that these myths no longer influence us.

Because these myths are so pervasive, it might be best to define and describe various aspects of male sexuality so you can explore your own attitudes and feelings about this aspect of your life. Sexuality is so complex and personal that it is impossible to capture everyone's experience in these short paragraphs. Ultimately, sexuality is based on communication and openness. These processes are useful no matter what your gender and sexual preference.

MEN IN THE SEXUAL ARENA

THE BEGINNINGS

Most psychologists believe that feelings of bodily pleasure are an important aspect of the human experience from birth to death. Although Freud (1925/1962) suggested that newborns experience sexual urges, it is widely believed that the tendency to enjoy touch is not a true sexual act, but more of an innocent natural sensual desire. Unfortunately, many children have had this innocent period of life intruded upon by adults who imposed negative judgments about self-exploration of the body and its pleasure. Others have damaged children by taking advantage of the sensual openness of the child to act out their adult sexual urges with children, who often experience psychological and sexual problems as they get older. While women report more experiences of sexual abuse in childhood, it is widely believed that many men also suffer from these actions. Because of the cultural taboo on appearing weak or vulnerable, most men block the experience out of consciousness or are afraid to ask for help even when they are aware of the event (Hunter, 1990).

In individuals who have not suffered abuse, conscious thoughts about sexual activity become most prevalent during adolescence, when the body is going through its hormonal changes. Accompanying the body's physical changes, which include a deepening of the voice, appearance of pubic hair, and a growth spurt, are increased feelings of attraction to members of the opposite sex. These feelings are expressed in sexual fantasy and the increasing frequency of erections. Most young men learn about masturbation, the stroking of the penis until it ejaculates semen, through self-exploration and from friends who describe or show each other how to do it (Abramson, 1973).

Frank, a 33-year-old psychotherapist, recalled this experience.

The most exciting thing that ever happened to me was to come for the first time. I had been looking at the girls in a copy of my dad's *Playboy* magazine, stroking myself, and all of a sudden I had this incredible feeling of pleasure. Then the white stuff started coming out of my penis and I thought, "Oh no, what's this stuff?" It felt so good that I did it as much as I could from then on.

While Frank describes an experience common to many men, most of us also felt a need to be quite secretive about this pleasurable act. For many men growing up in religious or sexually repressed households, masturbation was often associated with guilt and a feeling of being a bad person (Hass, 1979). Sorenson (1973) found that 45% of adolescent males who masturbated experienced some feelings of guilt and anxiety about it. While the negative effects of masturbation seem to arise from guilt, researchers have shown that the positive effects include providing a safe means of sexual experimentation, relieving sexual tension and generalized anxiety, and controlling the need to act out inappropriate sexual impulses (Masters, Johnson, & Kolodny, 1988a).

SEXUAL FANTASY AND REALITY

For a vast majority of men, sexual excitement in adolescence is accompanied by fantasy (Sorenson, 1973). The hardening of the penis is often associated with attractive females (or males) that are seen in magazines, television, movies, books, and at school. The content of the fantasy varies, but it invariably includes imitated versions of sexual activity with an imaginary partner. Although men may have a preference for male or female partners, it is not uncommon for heterosexual and homosexual men to have both hetero- and homosexual fantasies (Masters & Johnson, 1979). Accompanied by these fantasies, masturbation gives a man a strong, building physical pleasure that often results in orgasm. After ejaculation, the fantasy image usually disappears and for the time being sex is over. In adolescence it is common for young males to masturbate several times a day (Masters, Johnson, & Kolodny, 1988a). Nocturnal ejaculation, or "wet dream," is also a relatively common experience for many men (Kinsey, Pomeroy, & Martin, 1948).

When real encounters with potential sexual partners become possible, many men find that the initiation of sexual activity is more complicated than the fantasy. With little knowledge about how women become turned on, except what they read in books, hear in private conversations, or see in movies or videos, many men are unprepared for the close interpersonal contact a sexual encounter requires.

Randy, a 25-year-old man in counseling, recalled his first sexual experience as a lesson in humility.

> I went to the movies with this girl who I thought was attractive. I had fantasized a hot encounter in the privacy of my own bedroom. When it came to reality, I felt so nervous. Just putting my arm around her and obsessing on what to do next kept me from enjoying the movie. When we got out of the theater, we talked about everything except feelings we had toward each other or anything about sexuality. It made me realize that I didn't know what I was doing.

THE FEELING TABOO

As described in preceding chapters, the taboo on certain emotional states leaves men at a disadvantage in intimate relationships. Men have been conditioned to hide feelings of weakness, fear, confusion, and vulnerability and only permitted to show aggressiveness (including sexuality), anger, competitiveness, and control (Brannon, 1976). Making love often entails exposing our more tender feelings toward our partner. Having an emotional relationship would require us to let down our defenses and share our more vulnerable parts. Because this is so threatening, many men maintain their distance by either masturbating to fantasy images or by having excessively narcissistic sexual encounters that maintain their partners as sex objects (Zilbergeld, 1988).

Having sex while intoxicated or with a partner you have no other feeling for except sexual feelings may send a wrong signal to that person. Many women complain of men who have sex with them once and then end the relationship. It is not surprising that women as a group are often skeptical about male intentions and abstain from sexual activity until a more interpersonal relationship develops. As depicted in the prologue, men can also be the victims of sexual pursuit before a strong emotional relationship has been established. Although a one-night sexual encounter may provide short-term pleasure, it is often a poor substitute for the support, understanding, and love that men also crave but are often too afraid to ask for directly. Communicating with your partner about your feelings, intentions, and desires can make sexual activity more honest and genuine.

Dwayne, a 34-year-old musician, lamented,

I used to believe that having sex was what intimacy was all about. After several empty sexual encounters, I've come to realize that sex doesn't really fulfill me unless I feel comfortable enough with my partner to let her see who I really am beneath the surface.

THE SEX-MACHINE IDENTITY

Having accepted the definition of ourselves as sex machines, many men have performed the sex act even when they have had ambivalent or uncomfortable feelings about their sex partners or the current situation (Goldberg, 1976). The unwritten law that suggests that males are supposed to be ready and willing at any given time for a sexual encounter has increased performance anxiety and pushed us to betray our true feeling states. By accepting the sex machine as our identity, we diminish other aspects of ourselves that might also be important, such as how we are feeling, what we are thinking, and sensitivity to our changing sensory perceptions. The sex-machine identity also fails to take into account individual differences in our physiological functioning that might be a result of genetics, aging, or life circumstances. As a result we feel inadequate and impotent for not living up to the sexual ideal (Zilbergeld, 1988).

Enjoyable sex is most likely to occur in special situations. These include when both partners are relaxed and well rested; when there has been time to verbally share and enjoy each other's company; and when there has been a buildup of desire through gazing, talking, and touching. When these conditions are not met, sex is possible but not always as enjoyable. Sometimes it might be best to postpone sexual activity until you are more able to share time with your partner mentally and physically.

Kyle, a 37-year-old real estate developer in a men's group, responded to the question of when he enjoyed sex the most by saying, "When my wife and I are on vacation, our lovemaking is more intense and real than when we both have to be at work at eight every morning. We seem to be able to extend the passion all day and not worry about time or the future." Unfortunately, our life-styles do not always permit us to have free time to relax and enjoy each other. Under stressful circumstances, it is not unusual to use sex as a way to escape the stress and actually become relaxed.

Because the sex act involves two individuals, it is possible for one of you to be in the mood when the other is not. If a woman is not in the mood, it seems to be culturally acceptable for her not to engage in sexual activity. However, if a man is not in the mood, both he and his partner often think something is wrong. This societal double standard often encourages men to perform sexually when they are not fully motivated. While many men enjoy this "burden," others are plagued by a lack of desire or difficulty with ejaculation that leads them to feel shame at not being able to perform like a real man (Masters & Johnson, 1970).

SEX, PERFORMANCE, AND CONTROL

Trained from an early age to work hard at their pursuits, many men find that even making love can turn into an achievement endeavor (Keen, 1991). For these men, the final goals of sexual behavior include intercourse and orgasm. With these goals in mind, many men perfect techniques for getting women to go to bed with them. The initial flirting, the first phone call, the romantic date with flowers and an expensive dinner, listening with intent, and the uncritical tolerance for behaviors with which you might disagree are often steps that must be taken to get closer to the goal of making love.

Rather than let the relationship develop from the risks taken by both partners, many men find they must control the course of events. Aside from making the process more stressful, controlling the relationship in this way often stifles the partner's expression of uniqueness. She must conform to your stage setting; as a result she feels manipulated and controlled rather than loved and appreciated. Instead of having a fantasy evening resulting in sexual activity, the man often finds a cold, withdrawn partner who isn't on the same sexual wavelength.

Sydney, a 28-year-old female store manager, revealed, "I can tell when a man is going through an act to get me to bed from almost the instant we meet. I always hope that he'll drop the front so that I can get to know him and what's behind that charming mask. Unfortunately, this occurs only rarely."

Even when sexual activity begins, the male often continues to take charge to make sure that both he and his partner are sexually satisfied. Without much consultation, the man decides the sequence of sexual events, the pace of the process, the positions, and even how to best stimulate his partner. Unfortunately, even the most experienced and well read individual will still not know what his partner enjoys without communication and sensitivity. While many women become passive in response to this male superiority in the sexual arena, there are other women who want to communicate their wishes and even initiate and lead the sexual activity (Barbach, 1982). This can be especially disconcerting to the goal-oriented male who has not learned that he might also gain pleasure from being receptive to his partner in the sexual sphere.

The alternative to controlling the events is to change the focus to experiencing your partner in the present. Rather than working toward the goal of sex, enjoy the looking, the touching, the playfulness as significant events in themselves. Appreciate her style and ways that she tries to make contact with you. The looser and more comfortable you feel, the more this kind of energy will be communicated to your partner and the easier it will be for her to be with you. If each of you is turned on, physical touching and kissing might follow, but if you or your partner are hesitant, then either of you might choose not to take your contact any further. Sexual activity, if it occurs, will then be based on mutual feelings of attraction and desire, rather than on miscommunication or obligation.

MISINTERPRETATION OF TOUCH

A common problem among men is the misinterpretation of touch (Shotland & Craig, 1988). Often a casual or playful touch from a potential partner is thought to mean that sexual activity should follow. Rather than enjoying the touch in the moment, we have been taught to assume the openness is a sexual signal. This has led to uncomfortable moments between friends and partners where the sensual play becomes a sexual turn-on for the male. Many men have learned that there is aggressive touch and sexual touch, but they are uncomfortable with touch that carries other meanings. Hugging, cuddling, and holding may mean that one person needs closeness, security, or comfort, not sexual intercourse.

Walter, a 44-year-old college professor, stated, "I wasn't touched by my father at all and only occasionally hugged by my mother. The result has been that I am afraid to touch people because I don't know what they want. With women, I seem to always get a hard-on and feel sexual when I touch them, whether they mean it this way or not."

It is possible for hugging and kissing to be ends in themselves rather than a means toward sexual intercourse (Barbach, 1982). When you are open to the sensuality of your body you can experience pleasure without having to think ahead. By remaining in the present, you can fully sense stimulation and not feel pressured to follow a sexual script. Without distortion, you can clearly perceive the communication that is expressed in the touch, augment your perception with verbal explanation, and respond to the touch appropriately. With more understanding of touch, many men might get an opportunity to receive validation, support, acceptance, or love from a hug and feel relief that they do not have to make the gesture into a sexual one.

DATE RAPE

Some men emerge from a date that doesn't result in sex feeling resentful that after all their effort and expense there was no sexual payoff

(Muehlenhard, Friedman, & Thomas, 1985). Unfortunately, some men act out their anger. They decide they are going to get sex any way they can and actually commit date rape, forcing women into sexual activity against their will (Levine-MacCombie & Koss, 1986). Rape is an act of aggression and power by a man that ignores a woman's (or man's) right to decisions about her own body (Doyle, 1985). It has been said that the traditional male role of dominance over women actually encourages a climate for rape (Costin & Schwartz, 1987). Rape is never acceptable, even when you receive mixed messages from a woman. When she says "no," stop whatever you are doing. In this age, women are more likely to prosecute cases of attempted rape or acquaintance rape. A man can even be indicted for raping his wife (Finkelhor & Yllo, 1985). Ignorance of the rules in the sexual arena is not an excuse. Not only is there little satisfaction in engaging in sex with someone who doesn't want to have sex with you, but rape is both immoral and illegal.

HOW DO WOMEN ENJOY SEX?

Men have often been accused of thinking only of themselves during sexual activity (Hite, 1987). Focused on wanting to experience orgasm, they sometimes rush through the preliminary stages of sexual play. For many men, the hardening of the penis can occur rather quickly, while women are sexually aroused more slowly (Masters, Johnson, & Kolodny, 1988a). While a woman may have sexual hangups of her own, based on the mixed messages she receives about her body and her societal role, it is common for her to want to feel close and connected to her sexual partner (Zilbergeld, 1988). In contrast to the man, who is performance-oriented, the woman is often process-oriented. Her goal is not just to have an orgasm, but rather to enjoy the touching, the caressing, the kissing, and the verbal sharing that occur during the sexual encounter.

Juliana, a 29-year-old single woman, remarked:

Sex is not a contest or a heavy thing for me. I want to feel appreciated. I like men who take their time, kid around, and don't need to always be moving on to intercourse right away. One of my best sexual experiences was when my partner and I spent the whole night kissing, talking, and touching. We didn't even have intercourse that night.

It is not unusual to hear a woman say that she enjoys having interpersonal contact before having sex with a man. A large part of the turn-on for a woman is the fantasy of being with a man who can meet her emotional and intellectual, as well as physical, desires (Farrell, 1986). For many men, a woman's attractiveness often plays the greatest role in sexual excitement. With her needs often being more global and his more specific, a woman may try to experience as much of her fantasy as possible before allowing a man to become physical with her.

What this means is that a man must not only think of himself but also be aware of what his partner desires. Enjoying a woman's company by spending time with her in nonsexual ways often sends a message to her that you like her for who she is, not just because you want to have sex with her. When a woman believes that you see her as more than a sex object, she is more likely to allow herself to be vulnerable to you physically. Because many women are self-critical and uncomfortable with their own bodies, mainly due to their cultural upbringing, it is a significant step for them to allow you access to this private part of themselves (Barbach & Levine, 1980).

While it is important to be sensitive to a woman's needs, being too eager to please can also be a problem. Basing your self-worth on how well

Playfulness is an important element in a healthy sexual relationship.

you can turn a woman on can lead to disappointment when she doesn't have a fulfilling sexual experience. Rather than try to guess what a woman wants, ask her. The best sexual experiences will likely happen when both of you are communicating how you are feeling and what you want and are not solely focusing on achieving orgasm.

GAY MALE SEXUALITY

While many men are confused about their sexual identity, it has been taboo to discuss homosexual thoughts or feelings in public. With homophobia commonplace, it is difficult to explore one's sexual preferences without stirring up fear and anxiety in individuals who are threatened by the idea of men being with men in a sexual way. Many men wonder about gay sexuality and even experiment with it privately to confront their doubts and fears.

Some sex researchers conceptualize sexual preference as a continuum from exclusively heterosexual to partly hetero-homosexual to exclusively homosexual (Kinsey, Pomeroy, & Martin, 1948). Early psychoanalytic theories suggesting that men who have stern or absent fathers and overbearing mothers are more likely to become homosexual have proved to be unfounded (Doyle, 1989). Poor family relationships seem to result in various behavioral and personality manifestations, not just homosexuality. While the research is still inconclusive, there is evidence to suggest that a homosexual preference is not likely to have been psychologically or psychosocially induced, but rather is determined biologically (Bell, Weinberg, & Hammersmith, 1981). A majority of gay men, when interviewed by Bell, Weinberg, and Hammersmith (1981) acknowledged feeling different from their heterosexual peers even before puberty. Many wished that they could fit in with the other "straight" guys, but felt uneasy and dissatisfied in heterosexual relationships.

Tim, a 52-year-old gay college professor, revealed, "I knew I was different when I was 6 years old. I found myself looking at other boys and even being interested in the men's underwear section of the Sears catalog where there were male models. I didn't know I was gay, but as I look back, I knew there was something going on." While some gay men are "out of the closet" or public about their sexual preference, many gay men keep this aspect of themselves private because of society's prejudices.

Like heterosexuality in the late eighties, gay male sexuality in the early 1980s was changed drastically by the onset of the AIDS epidemic (Masters, Johnson, & Kolodny, 1988b). Sexual promiscuity was more common before the AIDS epidemic, but most gay men now practice safe sex.

Practicing safe sex means using condoms, being aware of a partner's sexual history, and taking responsibility for educating yourself about unsafe sexual practices such as unprotected anal intercourse or oral sex, or engaging in other high-risk behaviors. For some, it has meant abstaining from sex altogether because of the fear of contracting AIDS.

Masters and Johnson (1979) observed both straight and gay couples during sexual activity and found that kissing, holding, and the experiencing of orgasm were similar in both groups. They did find, however, that gay couples tended to take more time communicating, playing, and caressing before orgasm than did the men in heterosexual couples. A greater variety of stimulation techniques was also noted during gay sex. The frequency of sexual activity in long-term relationships has been found to be similar for both homosexual and heterosexual couples (Larson, 1982).

The mating rituals of gay men tend to revolve around socializing through friends and those who are part of the gay community. Because of a fear of being "outed," many gay men go to places where there are other available men, rather than trying to identify available partners in the heterosexual community (Marcuse, 1988). Like straight men with women, gay men are attracted to a man's appearance and his personality. Flirting through talking and eye contact is a means by which the men can assess their feelings about each other initially; then, through deeper sharing, they can become more comfortable with each other. In these times discussing protection from sexually transmitted diseases is an important prelude to sexual activity.

If you are concerned about your sexual preference and need to talk over how our are feeling, it is important to seek out a counselor or therapist who is open to the possibility of a man enjoying either a heterosexual or homosexual life-style. Hiding your confusion or fear often makes it worse because there is no outlet for your thoughts and feelings. Many men fear they are gay and just need some reassurance and feedback, while other men have a sense that they are gay and need encouragement and support to explore the possibility of this life-style (Muchmore & Hanson, 1991). Making the choice to come out even to himself is one of the most difficult steps any man can make. It takes a great deal of courage and support to establish a healthy gay identity in a primarily heterosexual culture.

PERSONAL VALUES AND CHOICES

Having sex is no longer a carefree experience because of the ever-present possibility of giving or receiving sexually transmitted diseases or impregnating your partner. Sexually transmitted diseases such as gonorrhea, syphillis, chlamydial infection, genital herpes, and acquired immune deficiency syndrome (AIDS) have made lovemaking a potentially painful and deadly activity. Making decisions about with whom and when to have sex, how to handle birth control, and what to do if your sexual partner gets pregnant has complicated an extremely pleasurable act. Each of us must be responsible enough to ourselves and our partners to think through the consequences before we choose to act.

PREVENTING AIDS

Acquired immune deficiency syndrome, more commonly known as AIDS, is currently the most feared sexually transmitted disease. The human immunodeficiency virus (HIV) gains access to the body through sexual activity (usually sexual intercourse with an infected partner), sharing an infected intravenous needle, or through an infected blood transfusion. Once inside the body, the virus attacks the T-helper cells, which are white blood cells that direct the body's immune system to fight infection. Copying genetic information from the T-cell, the virus produces new viruses that attack other T-cells and various parts of the immune system (Masters, Johnson, & Kolodny, 1988b).

Although some individuals have tested positive for the HIV virus and don't have symptoms, many others experience symptoms within two to eight years of being infected. The symptoms follow a degenerating pattern that eventually leads the body and mind to break down, resulting in death. Because you don't know whom someone else has slept with unless you ask, it is important to find out as much as you can about your sexual partner and his or her sexual history. Many couples take HIV tests before engaging in intercourse in order to be as safe as possible, but it is advisable to discuss the decision to be tested with a counselor or health professional. Doing so enables couples to be clear about each partner's motivations for testing and offers an opportunity to discuss implications of the results, whether they be positive or negative. Aside from abstaining from intercourse, using a latex condom during sexual activity, including oral sex, is thought to be the best prevention from most sexually transmitted diseases including AIDS. However, these diseases can be passed on by exchanging body fluids, so one should be careful about touching open cuts. If you are worried about catching AIDS or fear you might have been infected, don't hesitate to seek counseling with a health professional.

PREVENTING PREGNANCY

Aside from preventing a population explosion that will likely double the world's population in the next 30 years, birth control or contraception is a way to prevent unwanted pregnancy and have some control over family planning. While certain religions, such as Catholicism, forbid the use of contraception, most individuals enjoy the freedom to decide when and if they will bring children into the world.

Although it has been typical for society to make the woman responsible for birth control, many men now wish to make sure that they are protected as well from unwanted pregnancy and sexually transmitted diseases. It is sometimes difficult to stop when one is in the throes of passion to ask about birth control or to put on a condom, but the potential consequences often demand this type of action. It is not fair for the woman to be the only one to worry about pregnancy or disease since the man is also a responsible, participating partner.

Rick, a 21-year-old college student, admitted to being lax about contraception during some of his sexual encounters. "I am so excited that I don't want to stop the flow by dealing with birth control. I admit that I usually hope and expect that the woman has taken care of that. But I know with AIDS and other diseases I should care more. I'm not really ready to be a father and I always feel bad afterwards." Often, caring after the fact is too late. Direct communication not only helps you deal directly with the issue, but often opens up an intimate and caring dialogue with your partner.

UNEXPECTED PREGNANCY

Because birth control is not 100% effective and couples are not always careful, pregnancy can still occur. It is often a very painful and difficult decision to continue or terminate a pregnancy, especially when it is unexpected. Most of us are unprepared to make these kinds of decisions. We must search our souls and rely on our beliefs, feelings, values, and overall philosophy about life to guide us. Communication between the partners is essential, since optimally the decision is made as a result of heartfelt discussions between both of them.

Henry, a 22-year-old male, went along with his girlfriend's decision to terminate her pregnancy at nine weeks.

I was so frightened and unsure of what to do. I could think of the pros and cons of each side. For a week, I couldn't sleep thinking about the decision. When she told me she wanted to have an abortion, I supported her in it. The timing wasn't right. Neither of us were ready to settle down and have children yet. I believe in my heart that I'll get another chance to be a father when I am older and ready to welcome a child into my life.

Stephen, a 20-year-old male, decided with his girlfriend to sustain their unexpected pregnancy.

I was raised in a very religious household and believe that it is wrong to stop a baby from growing once it has been conceived. We decided to get married and make the commitment to this child to be the best parents we can be. My friends tell me I'm crazy, that I haven't "lived" yet. Maybe that's partially true, but I feel I am doing the right thing.

MAKING DECISIONS ABOUT SEX

For many individuals, the rules of sexual behavior have been defined by their families or religious upbringing. Even men raised with strong moral values have been given mixed signals about how they are to act sexually by our American culture. Teenagers are often not given explicit information about sex and are told they should wait to have sex until they are married or at least in a committed relationship (Gebhard, 1977). At the same time, the media portray sexuality as glamorous and exciting, while downplaying its potentially negative consequences. The general intolerance of homosexuality by our culture leaves those who are inclined to be homosexual without guidance or support, and our cultural inability to discuss sex openly inhibits any meaningful dialogue about how to make wise sexual decisions. It is no wonder that many of us are confused about our sexual values.

Your decision-making process about your sexual behavior should take into account your religious and moral values as well as the dynamics of the situation at hand. Think about the consequences of your actions and how they might impact your own and another's future. Sexual intercourse with a woman, even with contraception, opens the possibility of bringing life into the world. Intercourse without a condom means that you are risking not only pregnancy, but also sexually transmitted diseases. If you or your partner don't want to have sex for any reason, it is important for you to express these feelings and to have them respected. Good interpersonal communication between partners will help both of you make better choices about how and when to express your sexuality.

EPILOGUE

Since my experience with Ursula, I became a bit more cautious about jumping quickly into bed with a woman. In some ways it was easier to avoid intimacy by going to bed with a person right away. Experiencing physical intimacy before emotional intimacy has been established has often led me to feel empty following these types of sexual encounters. One woman I recall not even liking that much as a person, but it didn't matter because our relationship was based solely on sex.

In the era of AIDS, my sexual behavior changed even more radically. Having intercourse meant possible death, so I became even more careful. I recall awkward moments asking about past lovers and answering similar questions. Wearing a condom had to become a part of sexual play, or else there was a lingering fear that maybe this was the person from whom I might catch the AIDS virus. Several friends have experienced incredible sorrow, grief, and fear as their friends have been stricken by the disease. When Magic Johnson and Arthur Ashe, prominent professional athletes, announced they were HIV-positive, it sent a chill through me and many others I know. Let's hope we can find a cure in the near future. In the meantime, be careful out there. ■

SUMMARY

Because it is difficult to discuss sexuality openly in our culture, many men have become victims of word-of-mouth and media myths about what actually occurs during sex. It is important for each man to listen to his own feelings rather than act to impress or control another person. Men need to be able to differentiate between sensual and sexual touch and realize that sexual expression occurs best under conditions in which both partners feel safe and free to be themselves. In the current era, practicing safe sex is essential for the prevention of unwanted pregnancy and sexually transmitted diseases. It is important to remember that you are responsible for your sexual decisions and the consequences that may arise from them.

CONSCIOUSNESS-RAISING ACTIVITIES
ACTIVITY 1

Obtain several copies of some popular women's magazines such as *Cosmopolitan, Elle,* or *Glamour.* There are usually a number of articles in these publications that relate to sexuality. Write down the titles of any articles that address sexuality, and specifically male sexuality. Then spend some time discussing these titles and the expectations and myths that they imply. Do you agree with these attitudes? How do you feel about the behavior that these articles appear to prescribe for men?

ACTIVITY 2

In same-sex groups, take some time to compile a list of questions you always wanted to ask a member of the opposite sex. After you have finished, use these questions to stimulate discussion with members of the opposite sex. What do these questions tell us about sexual expectations? How do you feel about these expectations?

PERSONAL DEVELOPMENT EXERCISES
EXERCISE 1

Respond to the following items, and then use the responses for discussion. Use the following scale to respond:

> 5 = This statement is true most of the time.
> 4 = This statement is true much of the time.
> 3 = This statement is true some of the time.
> 2 = This statement is occasionally true.
> 1 = This statement is true almost none of the time.

_____ I feel that my sexual performance is an important way I can express my masculinity.

_____ I was made to feel guilty about expressing my sexuality growing up.

_____ My fantasies about sex are better than what happens in reality.

_____ I have made some bad choices in relationship partners by acting on my sexual urges only.

_____ I am the initiator of sex between myself and my partner.

_____ If I'm not having intercourse, I'm not satisfied sexually.

_____ I feel totally comfortable with masturbation.

_____ I fear that I might become impotent in the midst of engaging in sex.

_____ I have been criticized by my partner for rushing to intercourse.

_____ I feel guilty about fantasizing about sex with anyone other than my main sexual partner.

Go through your ratings and, in your journal, explain your responses. Where did these attitudes and values come from? Have you ever questioned the validity of your beliefs? What might you change after reading the chapter? As a possible consciousness-raising activity, go through these ratings with a trusted partner. Use the ratings as a way to talk about your sexual attitudes and values. If time permits, a general discussion about sexual attitudes might follow the dyad exercise.

EXERCISE 2
Use the space provided to answer the following questions.

1. Have you questioned your sexual identity? How did you resolve this confusion for yourself? If it hasn't been resolved, what might you do about it?

_____

_____

_____

_____

2. If you know that you are gay, how have you handled the stresses that go with being an unaccepted minority in a heterosexual culture?

_____

_____

_____

_____

3. If you are straight, how have you dealt with the existence of gay men? Have you been guilty of stereotyping or making fun of these men? How do you understand your behavior if you have been negative or critical of gays?

_____

_____

_____

_____

EXERCISE 3

These questions might stimulate discussion about safe sex and the changes that have occurred in attitudes about sex because of sexually transmitted diseases.

1. How have sexually transmitted diseases affected your sexual practices and the way you live your life?

_____

_____

_____

_____

2. How might you treat a friend who has been infected by a sexually transmitted disease? How would you want to be treated?

_____

_____

_____

_____

3. What information would you like to have about sexually transmitted diseases in order to be more responsible for your sexual health?

_____

_____

_____

_____

REFERENCES

ABRAMSON, P. R. (1973). The relationship of the frequency of masturbation to several aspects of behavior. *Journal of Sex Research, 9,* 132–142.

BARBACH, L. G. (1982). *For each other: Sharing sexual intimacy.* Garden City, NY: Anchor Press.

BARBACH, L. G., & LEVINE, L. (1980). *Shared intimacies.* Garden City, NY: Anchor Press.

BELL, A. P., WEINBERG, M. S., & HAMMERSMITH, S. K. (1981). *Sexual preference: Its development in men and women.* Bloomington: Indiana University Press.

BRANNON, R. (1976). The male sex role: Our culture's blueprint of manhood, and what it's done for us lately. In D. David & R. Brannon (Eds.), *The forty-nine percent majority: The male sex role* (pp. 1–45). Reading, MA: Addison-Wesley.

COSTIN, F., & SCHWARTZ, N. (1987). Beliefs about rape and women's social roles: A four-nation study. *Journal of Interpersonal Violence, 2,* 45–56.

DOYLE, J. (1985). *Sex and gender.* Dubuque, IA: William C. Brown.

DOYLE, J. (1989). *The male experience.* Dubuque, IA: William C. Brown.

FARRELL, W. (1986). *Why men are the way they are.* New York: McGraw-Hill.

FINKELHOR, D., & YLLO, K. (1985). *License to rape: Sexual abuse of wives.* New York: Holt, Reinhart & Winston.

FREUD, S. (1962). *Three essays on the theory of sexuality*. (J. Strachey, Trans.). New York: Basic Books. (Originally published in 1925.)

GEBHARD, P. H. (1977). The acquisition of basic sex information. *Journal of Sex Research, 13,* 148–169.

GOLDBERG, H. (1976). *The hazards of being male*. New York: New American Library.

HASS, A. (1979). *Teenage Sexuality*. New York: Macmillan.

HITE, S. (1987). *Women and love: A cultural revolution in progress*. New York: Knopf.

HUNTER, M. (1990). *Abused boys: The neglected victims of sexual abuse*. New York: Ballantine Books.

KEEN, S. (1991). *Fire in the belly: On being a man*. New York: Bantam Books.

KINSEY, A. C., POMEROY, W. B., & MARTIN, C. E. (1948). *Sexual behavior in the human male*. Philadelphia: Saunders.

LARSON, P. (1982). Gay male relationships. In W. Paul, J. Weinrich, J. Gonsiorek, & M. Hotvedt (Eds.), *Homosexuality: Social, psychological and biological issues* (pp. 219–232). Beverly Hills, CA: Sage.

LEVINE-MACCOMBIE, J., & KOSS, M. (1986). Acquaintaince rape: Effective avoidance strategies. *Psychology of Women Quarterly, 10,* 311–320.

MARCUSE, E. (1988). *The male couple's guide to living together. What gay men should know about living together and coping in a straight world*. New York: Harper & Row.

MASTERS, W. H., & JOHNSON, V. E. (1970). *Human sexual inadequacy*. Boston: Little, Brown.

MASTERS, W. H., & JOHNSON, V. E. (1979). *Homosexuality in perspective*. Boston: Little, Brown.

MASTERS, W. H., JOHNSON, V. E., & KOLODNY, R. C. (1988a). *Human sexuality*. Glenview, IL: Scott, Foresman.

MASTERS, W. H., JOHNSON, V. E., & KOLODNY, R. C. (1988b). *Crisis: Heterosexual behavior in the age of AIDS*. New York: Grove Press.

MUCHMORE, W., & HANSON, W. (1991). *Coming out right: A handbook for the gay male*. Boston: Alyson.

MUEHLENHARD, C., FRIEDMAN, D., & THOMAS, C. (1985). Is date rape justifiable? The effects of dating activity, who initiated, who paid, and men's attitudes toward women. *Psychology of Women Quarterly, 9,* 297–310.

SHOTLAND, R., & CRAIG, J. (1988). Can men and women differentiate between friendly and sexually interested behavior? *Social Psychology Quarterly, 51,* 66–73.

SORENSON, R. C. (1973). *Adolescent sexuality in contemporary America*. New York: World.

ZILBERGELD, B. (1988). *Male sexuality: A guide to sexual fulfillment*. Boston: Little, Brown.

SUGGESTED READINGS

BARBACH, L. G. (1982). *For each other: Sharing sexual intimacy.* Garden City, NY: Anchor Press.

BIERY, R. E. (1990). *Understanding homosexuality: The pride and the prejudice.* Austin, TX: William.

DUBERMAN, M. B., VICINUS, M., & CHAUNCEY, G. (Eds.). (1989). *Hidden from history: Reclaiming the gay and lesbian past.* New York: Penguin Books.

HITE, S. (1981). *The Hite report on male sexuality.* New York: Knopf.

HUNTER, M. (1990). *Abused boys: The neglected victims of sexual abuse.* New York: Ballantine Books.

MASTERS, W. H., JOHNSON, V. E., & KOLODNY, R. C. (1988). *Crisis: Heterosexual behavior in the age of AIDS.* New York: Grove Press.

MUCHMORE, W., & HANSON, W. (1991). *Coming out right: A handbook for the gay male.* Boston: Alyson.

REID, J. (1976). *The best little boy in the world.* New York: Ballantine Books.

REINISCH, J. M. (1990). *The Kinsey Institute new report on sex: What you must know to be sexually literate.* New York: St. Martin's Press.

SPARK, R. F. (1991). *Male sexual health.* Mt. Vernon, NY: Consumer Reports Books.

ZILBERGELD, B. (1988). *Male sexuality.* Boston: Little, Brown.

CHAPTER 6

MEN AT WORK

Upon finishing ninth grade I landed a job working on an all-purpose labor crew for a private boarding school in my hometown. Summer was the time to clean the dorm rooms, paint the walls, repair the roofs, clean out the swimming pool filter, and mow the grounds. Each crew was supervised by an older man who was a career employee of the school.

Over the course of the summer a quiet competition emerged among us boys. The competition involved knowing who among us could loaf with the best of them, and who could work hard with the best of them. There was a great deal of pride to be won in each camp. After being assigned a task for the day, the loafers would take off in search of a secluded hiding place where they would set up camp with pop, candy, cigarettes, and a radio. Our work stations were always within easy reach, and when a supervisor would come to monitor our progress, we would spring to work immediately and appear to be getting something done. Looking back, it is amazing that we thought we were fooling our superiors. At the end of the day we took pride in the fact that we had spent the full eight hours, the six of us, accomplishing what could probably have been done by one man in about a half hour. And to top it off, we got paid for a full eight-hour day.

The hard-working camp would be assigned to tasks such as painting the roof of the classroom building or tearing shingles off the administration building. This work was hard and demanding and more difficult to slough off because the hard workers were usually assigned to the more demanding supervisors. We would take only the scheduled breaks, work hard, set a fast pace, and strive to do our best even when it hurt. But at the end of the day, when we came back to the shed after a long, sweaty, grueling eight hours, we knew we had accomplished a lot. It showed in our sweaty brows, dirty hands, gritty clothes, and dark tans. Over the summer we came to recognize which camp we belonged in, the workers or the sloughers. Although unspoken, each of us experienced the unmistakable emergence of an identity that would shape our view of ourselves as workers for the rest of our lives. ■

INTRODUCTION: THE CHANGING FACE OF WORK

In the not-too-distant past, men were primarily socialized to be the breadwinners. A man would get up in the morning, leave home, work hard each day, "bring home the bacon," and leave the burden of homestead responsibilities to his domestic partner. Men defined themselves almost exclusively by their work. A man's identity became intimately related to his work and the particular economic and social strata in which he situated himself through his job. A man's work, his place in society, had a far-reaching impact on his friendships, social relations, and opportunities.

Men in today's culture have many more options regarding their choice of work roles and the meaning of work in their lives than their fathers or grandfathers. As women's roles changed dramatically during the last half of the 20th century, men's options have increased. Women have entered the paid labor force in increasing numbers. Men have crossed the boundary into what was previously considered women's work. A man in today's world cannot assume the simple, secure roles of the past.

The addition of women to the work force, and the new and diverse roles this offers for both men and women, have affected men's lives in several other domains as well. Men's relationships with other men and women have evolved. Relationships in which both partners work create new demands and challenges for each person as opportunities arise for one and not the other. Women's success in the world of work creates new possibilities for couples who choose to have children. The couple might decide it's more appropriate for the male to stay home and rear the children because he wishes to or because the woman earns more money. The simplicity of men's and women's roles in the past has been replaced by a complex, challenging, and ultimately richly rewarding world in which to define yourself, your life, and your values through work.

MEN AND THE WORK IDENTITY

As men, we have received distinct messages about the importance of work in our lives. Many people in our culture tend to equate a man's work identity with who he is; therefore, it is not unusual for new acquaintances to ask, "What kind of work do you do?" before any other information is exchanged. Others, including potential mates, often judge a man's earning potential as a significant indicator of his ability to be a good provider (Gould, 1974). Many men derive their self-esteem directly from how they and others value what they do in the world of work (Skovholt, 1990).

To men who perceive work as more than just a way to earn money or gain status, career accomplishment offers the opportunity to fulfill a powerful need to make a difference in the world. The career as a calling represents a personal, individual investment in one's work. Men who enjoy their work find themselves interested, stimulated, and motivated by what they do (Weiss, 1990). While this commitment and investment often pay handsome dividends in self-esteem, status, and security, these dividends are not always the prime motivators. Unfortunately, work can also become such an obsession that some men begin to avoid other aspects and responsibilities in their lives.

What makes some men define themselves solely by their job status? Why is it so important that a man be the breadwinner or provider? How is it that some men find meaning and enjoyment in their work while others struggle just to make work tolerable for themselves? What happens to the man who becomes obsessed with his work?

THE COMPETITIVE ANGLE

In our competitive economic system, very few individuals reach the pinnacle of success. There always seems to be someone who is better at what he does or who earns more, so even successful men don't feel fully satisfied with themselves (Berglas, 1986). Competition is encouraged early in a man's development. Many boys are encouraged to compete in athletics as a way of learning how to make it in the real world (Kohn, 1986). Others compete so they can gain the perceived rewards of being a winner (Messner, 1987). It is common in our culture for a winner to be acknowledged and admired, while losers are ignored or ridiculed. Boys who fail to find an arena where they can be a winner often feel a sense of shame and low self-esteem as they compare themselves to their peers (Eitzen, 1975; Fasteau, 1974).

As boys develop into men, the world of work becomes the arena for competition. The underlying assumption of a competitive system is that the strongest will thrive. While physical strength might be important in pro-

fessional sports or in construction jobs, it is not necessary in many work settings today. With only a tiny minority of athletes making it into high-paying professional sports careers, many former athletes must retool in order to compete in the world of work (Messner, 1987). Ironically, some of the boys who once were losers on the playground are now the winners in the workplace because their cognitive abilities are valued by the culture. Just as in childhood, the winners gain prestige and status; as adults, they also gain financial reward. The losers must struggle with feelings of inadequacy as they try to find a sense of identity in the workplace. This type of problem has been described by social scientists who have studied underprivileged African-American men who unrealistically modeled their aspirations on professional athletes and entertainers portrayed in the media. Since only a tiny minority of individuals are able to attain success in these professions, many of these young men are left without the knowledge, skills, or guidance to succeed in the workplace (Messner, 1992; Parham & McDavis, 1987).

Steve, a 38-year-old ex-athlete, is still trying to find success in his life after sports.

> I used to love overpowering my competition with bursts of speed and grace, but now I am finding that I am the slow one. I wish that I had taken school more seriously so I could compete out in the business world. Right now I'm taking a remedial writing course so I can move up from the position I am in with my company. Just being ordinary has been real troubling to me. I want to shine and be seen as important, but right now that is just a fantasy.

THE PROVIDER ROLE

While not all men can be winners, many of those who work experience satisfaction when they bring home a paycheck and provide for themselves and their families. Since the industrial revolution, when men left the home to go to work, a man's reward for working long hours under severe conditions has been knowing he could provide for his family (Bernard, 1981). Economic survival continues to be a motivating factor for men to work even when they dislike or find little pleasure in their jobs. Not being able to provide for themselves or their families is seen by many men as confirmation that they are failures as men (Pleck, 1975). Hard economic times that bring a slowdown in work, lower salaries, and layoffs also bring increases in depression. Men, who have traditionally defined themselves by their ability to be breadwinners, may be particularly vulnerable (Ross & Huber, 1985).

The influx of women into the workplace in the last 20 years has

changed the meaning of breadwinning. Since almost two-thirds of married women work outside the home, the breadwinner role has become a less important symbol of masculinity than it once was. Many households depend on two salaries for a higher standard of living or even for mere economic subsistence; earning an income is also a means for women to feel valued and respected (Doyle, 1989). Men are adjusting slowly to the reality that working in stereotypically male environments is not solely a masculine activity. They are also learning to value the domestic chores and child care they must share with their spouses in two-career families as an expanded definition of what it means to be a man (Cowan & Bronstein, 1988).

Otto, a 26-year-old construction worker who has been having trouble finding steady work during a recent recession, feels ashamed of his diminished earning power.

> I always thought that I would earn enough money to take care of myself, my kid, and my wife. Lately, I've been the one staying home and my wife has been getting us by with her salary. It's hard for me not to feel down about my situation. I'm embarrassed not to be working and bringing home a paycheck. I like coming home at the end of the day knowing I've earned enough to pay our rent, put food on the table, and have enough left over to take my wife out to dinner and the movies on the weekend.

GAINING MEANING FROM WORK

Aside from trying to prove yourself a winner and providing for your family, work can also be interesting and meaningful. Men who enjoy their jobs often find deeper meaning in their work that encourages them to pursue it with a sense of mission and purpose (Weiss, 1990). It is not common for a man to say that he loves the challenge or can't wait to solve the next problem that comes up when he has found a vocation that matches his interests and values. Unfortunately, many men find their jobs meaningless and disconnected from what gives them pleasure (Terkel, 1975). While many jobs are inherently uninteresting, it seems that it is our responsibility to make them meaningful and enjoyable. Since the average man spends 70% of his life at work, it seems important that his job give him some sense of satisfaction.

It has been said that the attitude one takes into the job has a direct influence on how a man experiences his work (Fields, Taylor, Weyler, & Ingrasci, 1984). A man who puts little effort into learning and understanding what he is doing may find that his job holds little meaning for him. In

contrast, the man who decides to learn all about his work, including how it is impacting others, may be in a better position to evaluate what he does. The job itself might be boring, but he might find enjoyment in communicating with his peers or using the time to think and ponder what is important to him. Castaneda's (1968) character Don Juan reminds us that if a man is to be satisfied with his life including his work, he must pursue a path that has a heart. If a job doesn't fit a man's personality or has no value for him aside from picking up a paycheck, he may need to look into other work possibilities that challenge him enough to sustain him.

Bill, a 32-year-old engineer, describes the meaning of work in his life:

> I was programmed from an early age to do well in school, and to get good grades. Success was everything. When I graduated from college, it was onto the fast track. Up, up, and away I went in the engineering firm I joined. It was easy. But after a few years I began to feel there was something more to life that I wasn't getting. Was this all there was? I took off some time and realized that I was not being true to myself at work. I was helping design the communication systems in fighter jets. I didn't want to contribute to the destruction of the planet so I switched jobs and now work in a small engineering firm that is designing alternative energy products. I enjoy doing to work and doing what I believe in.

DANGERS OF THE WORK OBSESSION

When a man views his work as the main, or only, means of articulating his masculine identity, he is in danger of becoming work obsessed. A man who is not gratified by home life, hobbies, or activities outside of the work environment can find sanctuary at his job. The workaholic is often a driven individual who works to the exclusion of other enjoyable life activities. A workaholic is characterized by fears of failure, anxiety about the future, irritation with others who are not work obsessed, and a belief that one should live to work rather than work to live (Fassel, 1990). It is not uncommon for this type of man to alienate family, friends, and loved ones while undermining his physical and mental health.

To the work-obsessed man, work becomes an addictive substance used in much the same way as alcohol or cocaine. The man experiences some immediate pleasure from the work, but this pleasure is rarely from the work itself but rather from the relief he obtains by avoiding stress, commitment, intimacy, life problems, or other issues. It is not unusual for the extreme workaholic to eventually burn out in the form of emotional and physical collapse from his addiction since he does not nurture himself or find alternative outlets for his energy (Freudenberger & Richelson, 1980).

Victor, a 41-year-old man in individual counseling, recalls the nature of his work obsession.

> I started out my career as a scientist thinking that I had found the ultimate way to enjoy life. I worked on several parallel projects trying to discover the nature of certain types of genetic material. I loved going into the lab and eventually began to stay there evenings and weekends. I had no social life, no contact with others except for my assistants who were there normal working hours. Eventually I started feeling run down and depressed. I didn't know what to do. It wasn't until I literally collapsed one night and was found in the morning by my assistant that I had started to see the nature of my obsession. I was admitted to a hospital, transferred to the psychiatric ward, and eventually began putting the pieces back together with the help of a sensitive therapist.

Many men who are susceptible to workaholism need to find other outlets for their energy. In the cutthroat atmosphere of certain competitive work environments, there are few places to escape stress. It is important to find outside interests unrelated to work to allow for releases of energy, playfulness, and emotional renewal. Like other addictions, workaholism is not easily changed. It takes a concerted effort and often the help of friends, a counselor, or a self-help group to change this type of behavior pattern.

THE INFLUENCE OF THE MALE GENDER ROLE ON CAREER DECISION MAKING

Research has shown that matching a job to a person's interests, values, and abilities will have a direct relation to how satisfied he is with his work, how positive his job performance is, whether he might advance in the chosen career or job, and how he feels about himself as a person within a certain career field (Holland, 1985). Men's interests, values, and abilities are impacted by male gender role biases (Skovholt, 1990). Men with more traditional views of masculinity are likely to restrict their choices based on how well a potential career fits with their own image of themselves as men. Such men often favor work settings that allow them to compete, accomplish, demonstrate competency, and be in power over settings that are more social and female oriented (Crites & Fitzgerald, 1978). Even so, some men are beginning to cross the boundary into stereotypically female careers.

WHAT INTERESTS MEN?

Interests are understood as affinities and preferences for various activities that affect a choice of a job or career. Holland (1966; 1985) proposed a typology of interests that defines six different interest clusters: realistic, investigative, artistic, social, enterprising, and conventional. These six interest clusters correspond to six personality types, and Holland's theory is that people of distinct personality types gravitate to work environments that correspond to these interest patterns.

The traditional male role tends to lead men toward realistic, investigative, and enterprising interests. It is not unusual for many men to have watched their fathers work on cars, fix the plumbing, or make home repairs. With father as a role model and one who reinforces this type of interest in his son by attending to him during these occasions, many men seem to gravitate toward fields that allow them to be realistic and physical and to work with their hands. Investigative interests have also been encouraged by parents and teachers. The autonomous, logical process of figuring out how things work has also been traditionally seen as a masculine activity that boys seem to be reinforced for more than girls. As adults, men have followed their interest in logic to dominate fields such as engineering, medicine, and law. Enterprising interests have also been included in the male domain. Because of the emphasis on being autonomous, in charge, and in control of their destiny, it is not uncommon for men to choose to go into business settings with the ultimate ideal of owning and running their own enterprise. This fits well with the American masculine stereotype of being a self-made man (Gerzon, 1982).

Although men go into other fields, the standard upbringing in our culture has encouraged them to be attracted to realistic, investigative, and enterprising careers. Artistic, social, and conventional interests, expressed through such occupations as teaching or secretarial work, often are either discouraged or only mildly encouraged, leading men with these interests to feel unsupported. While some males continue to follow nontraditional interests, many men give up these options and settle for the traditional path that might not bring them as much joy or pleasure as their true interests.

Ethan, a 22-year-old business student, is still struggling with what he would like to do with his work life.

> I have always enjoyed acting and being around the theater. When I mentioned this to my father, he told me that I probably wouldn't make it in that field. He also said he wouldn't fund my college if I decided to major in theatre. So here I am majoring in business but

knowing in my heart that I would love to give acting a try. I'm not sure what I'm going to do.

VALUES MEN BRING TO CAREER DECISIONS

Values are the guiding principles, beliefs, and attitudes to which a person refers when making decisions. Values have a personal and very strong meaning for most of us. As we develop more life experience and are exposed to different situations in life, we affirm or revise our values. Men learn their values through family, school, education, and the media in our culture. Like interests, values are influenced by gender role socialization (O'Neil & Fishman, 1986).

David and Brannon (1976) suggest that men are influenced by four basic values related to masculinity: the big wheel, the sturdy oak, give 'em hell, and no sissy stuff. The big wheel is symbolic of the masculine value of being important, successful, and in charge. Men who embrace these values tend to gravitate toward careers that give them an opportunity to have status or to be the boss, such as careers in business or the professions. The sturdy oak represents the masculine ideal of toughness, self-reliance, and confidence. Many men enter occupations that allow them to display fearlessness, make life-or-death decisions, and rely on physical strength, such as police work or construction work. Give 'em hell values dangerousness, aggressiveness, and power that can be found in the military; professional athletics such as football, boxing, and hockey; and thrill-seeking activities that might occur outside the work environment. No sissy stuff is a traditional masculine value that prohibits men from showing affection or appearing feminine in any way. Careers as teachers, artists, counselors, or nurses may be discouraged because of this antifeminine value.

Greg, a 40-year-old high school teacher, recalls his struggle with career choice because of conflicting values.

> I always thought that I'd be a policeman or fireman. I loved action. While most of my friends from our lower middle-class neighborhood got jobs out of high school, I decided to go to college. I was surprised at my reaction to this setting. I really enjoyed learning and found my professors to be impressive in their ability to get up in front of the room and teach. I emulated one in particular and now can't think of anything I'd rather be doing.

A MAN NEEDS ABILITY

If a man has an interest in but not the ability for a certain vocation, it is unlikely that he will succeed. Abilities are a result of both natural endowment and learned skills. Throughout our schooling a major emphasis is placed on abilities, both intellectual and social, for success. At an early age little boys begin to define themselves through their perceptions of their abilities. Athletic ability, street smarts, and social ability are all important ways the growing boy defines who he is. Self-confidence is directly related to this personal recognition of competence. As adults, however, a greater emphasis is placed on intellectual and academic ability as the prerequisites for success and achievement in our culture. In addition, perseverance, social savvy, and leadership skills make a man competitive in the workplace. Men who are willing to learn new skills are more likely to find work that is satisfying and rewarding. Men who have an unrealistic perception of their abilities may be unable to find jobs in their desired fields or work in jobs that don't fit their image of themselves. With the world economy moving toward a service and information emphasis, men who are unwilling to adapt to the changing landscape of needed work skills will find themselves less qualified for the jobs of the future (Naisbitt, 1984).

Antoine, a 49-year-old bricklayer in career counseling, is facing the conflict of having to find a new career after suffering a debilitating back injury. "I have done the same job for 30 years. I knew this day would come when I had to give up physical labor, but I don't know what I'm interested in or even what else I'd be good at. Who would want to hire a 49-year-old high school dropout anyway?"

NONTRADITIONAL CAREER CHOICES

As stated earlier, many men refuse to consider career options they see as feminine or unmanly. Men have also been channeled away from stereotypically feminine careers by school counselors and teachers (Stanworth, 1983). Traditionally, female-dominated careers have paid less and yielded lower status, which makes them less attractive to men, who are socialized to value status and financial reward highly (Bridges, 1989).

In this era when women have broken barriers to the male workplace, men have an opportunity to extend their career possibilities by doing work that has not been traditionally in the masculine province. While many men still hesitate to consider careers in the arts, nonphysician health care, elementary school teaching, library science, or secretarial and data processing work, more men are crossing over into these fields (Wegmann, Chapman, & Johnson, 1989). Men who have interests, values, and abilities in nontraditional areas are beginning to follow their inclinations. They are finding more acceptance among their coworkers in female-dominated settings than women are finding in male-dominated settings (Fine, 1987).

Jarret, a 25-year-old male nurse, describes his experience in a hospital setting:

> I enjoy my job and feel that I do it well. The other nursing staff, who are all female, accept me personally and professionally. I have had the hardest time from some of the male patients who complain that they want a "real nurse" who they characterize as female. There have been times when some of my patients mistake me for a physician because I'm male.

TRADITIONAL STAGES OF MALE CAREER DEVELOPMENT

It is into the context of economic necessity and evolving, changing cultural expectation that men are born and raised. How will a man embody his identity and values through his choice of an occupation? What influences his choices? How does a man's family and his upbringing influence his choices? What other kinds of influences might a man consider as he engages in the exciting yet challenging task of choosing work and finding meaning in the work he has chosen?

These messages, clearly not always positive or consistent, combine with parental role models, self-knowledge, interests, abilities, values, and information about the world of work to produce a choice of work role or career. A number of social scientists have investigated how men choose careers. Two ways of looking at a man's approach to career choice have evolved from these studies. One approach focuses on the various stages a person negotiates as he or she arrives at a career choice and how these choices are maintained or reconsidered over the life span. The second approach focuses on the individual's attributes that factor into a specific career or occupational choice.

Roe and Lunneborg (1990), Ginzberg (1972), Tiedeman and O'Hara (1963), and Super (1984, 1990) have all studied the stages through which a person passes as he or she establishes a career. Although diverse in the language they use to describe these stages, there is some agreement among them that an occupation or career represents a series of choices that unfold over time based on an individual's values, abilities, and developing self-concept or personality. They have identified some broad, yet distinguishable stages of career development. These include the fantasy and exploration, tentative choice, establishment, maintenance, and decline stages.

For many men, the earliest elements of the career choice process involve early childhood curiosities, fantasies, and daydreams about future work roles. Watching and listening to male role models as well as being exposed to male socialization messages through the media influence the little boys' notions about work and careers. This is called the fantasy or exploration stage of career development. For example, many young boys daydream about becoming a fireman or a policeman or a doctor. Little boys' toys are manufactured to capitalize on this natural inclination to fantasize about these roles and to provide opportunities for little boys to enact their developing ideas about what work and working mean to him personally.

The exploration stage evolves further when the little boy leaves the home environment and enters school. As he moves through grammar school, elementary school, junior high school, and high school, his thinking about careers and work becomes more complex and sophisticated. Through feedback from teachers, he learns about himself and his abilities and values. Through observation he learns about the world of work and about what certain occupations actually require. He begins an early selection process by exploring different career paths, learning the requirements of these paths, and getting to know his own abilities and endowments, which will necessarily limit some paths and make others seem natural. As a result, he selects some occupations as possibilities and rejects others.

By the time a young man enters and then graduates from high school, he has some emerging sense of himself and who he wants to be in

Adult career choice often has its beginnings in childhood play, fantasy, and daydreams.

terms of a career. He will have made a tentative selection of a career. He makes choices about advanced education, job training, apprenticeship, or other kinds of work experiences and begins a more concrete and definite implementation of his ideas about a career. He may begin one career, find it lacking for him, change to another related career, or plan to switch to an entirely new direction.

Upon the completion of secondary education, or perhaps advanced educational or career training, the young man is prepared to enter the world of work. He has made a commitment to a vocation and is now prepared to apply his knowledge, skills, and expertise in society and to receive financial compensation for his work. He will make a more definite commitment to a career or occupation. He will stabilize in this work, advance, and continue on the path of career development. Or he may find the work frustrating and reconsider his choice.

More recently, a number of social scientists have extended these notions about career choice and vocational development into adulthood. Levinson et al. (1978) and Gould (1978) have extended thinking about career development and adult development beyond the stage of initial career choice and maintenance. These authors give voice to the struggle that many men experience about the personal meaning of work and career in their lives across their lifespans. While traditional theories have emphasized the notion that one chooses a career and begins a linear trajectory through it, these theorists find that in their middle years men become intensely involved in questioning the value of their work and their commitment to it.

Young adulthood takes up where many of the earlier theories about career development leave off—that is, at the time in the early 20s when a man enters the adult world, the work force, and begins to establish a career as well as a new stage of identity for himself. The themes of early adulthood relate to entering an occupation, setting up a home base away from the family of origin, and making early decisions about relationships and potential partners in life. The young man creates a new life structure for himself in these realms in his early to middle 20s and then tries them out to see how they work for him. In the late 20s and early 30s, a number of men experience what has been called the "Age 30 Transition," during which they question the choices they made when they entered the adult world and reaffirm or change them. This reconsideration of choices in the 30s usually leads to a period of stability that may last into middle adulthood, the late 40s or early 50s.

Stu, a 32-year-old man who began working in the food and beverage industry right out of college, realized he wasn't satisfied with his career choice.

> I became tired of the same old routine. I wasn't growing. I always had the fantasy of becoming a lawyer so I made up my mind to study for the LSATs and to my surprise, I did well enough to get accepted into law school. This time around, I was motivated to study and I graduated at the top of my class. Now I love the challenges of my work. I'm so glad I went with my dream.

Middle adulthood is usually preceded by the midlife transition during which the choices of early adulthood are questioned and challenged. The meaning of work, and the other life choices a man made are sometimes called into question as discontent, disillusionment, and boredom begin to surface in his experience. He contemplates changes, makes plans and carries through. In the process he may change jobs, relationships, and geographic locations.

Another choice a man may make is to affirm the earlier choices and recommit himself to their value and meaning (Weiss, 1990). Often a man in this stage will obtain gratification from mentoring a younger protégé, assisting him or her with the challenges of the job based on his own personal experience and insight. As a man makes these changes or recommits to initial choices, he becomes comfortable in middle adulthood with his choices and acknowledges the value of them. This is a more or less settled down period of life in which a man frequently continues to advance at work, reestablishes relationships within his own family that may have been compromised during his earlier focus on career advancement, and begins to find ways to balance his work and family experiences.

Frank, a 50-year-old public relations vice-president, said:

> I thought about quitting several times, but I wasn't sure what else I would do. I finally realized that even though I don't always enjoy my work, my family and friends are what is most important. I'm used to my job and have accepted its limitations. I have also become interested in acting as a mentor, showing some of the younger folks what I wish someone had showed me.

Of course, some men may have greater challenges to face in their middle adult years. A history of failed career endeavors or personal relationships may have mounted up and now demands some understanding. Distance between the man and his family, sometimes caused by his allowing his work pursuits to become his primary focus, may have become so great that a divorce or family estrangement must be accepted. A man's own family of origin may be beginning to disintegrate, leaving him vulnerable to an even greater sense of loneliness and isolation if he has not established a family for himself in his early adulthood years. The middle adult years can be very challenging for many men; they must now accept the consequences of the choices they made. These choices may have given the man an apparent advantage early in his life, but now, as he looks back and wonders what happened, he may see his earlier choices as nearsighted or lacking in lasting value.

Late adulthood is characterized by disengaging from work and taking stock of the choices you made throughout your life. Retirement is often a difficult transition for a man who has defined himself by his work (Parnes, 1981). Depression and feelings of meaninglessness accompany retirement for men who have not found relationships, hobbies, and leisure activities to replace the time spent at work (Fillenbaum, George, & Palmore, 1985).

As a man begins to wind down his career, his relationships with family members, partners, and friends evolve and mature. He may contemplate his own contributions to others' lives and develop a feeling of what Erik Erikson (1982) called *integrity*. He may then feel his life has had meaning and his work has made a positive and valuable contribution.

Not every man's life follows the clearly delineated patterns and progressions just described. However, these stages of development are usually found in research as well as in clinical and counseling work with men (Skovholt & Morgan, 1981). The issues raised in these stages are important. The challenges of setting up an adult work life and the challenges of evaluating and reevaluating one's choices are common themes in counseling men and in discussions in men's groups.

DUAL-CAREER PARTNERSHIPS

In recent years, it has become quite common for women to be in the workplace. As women have moved into career tracks and positions that were previously male dominated, men have had to adjust as coworkers and as spouses to this reality (Pleck, 1985). Men raised with traditional gender roles have had the most difficulty with the transition since it runs against their expectations of the woman's place in the family. It has meant that a man can no longer expect that his wife will spend the day at home cleaning house and taking care of the kids (Gilbert, 1987).

For most men the presence of women in the workplace has meant altering their behavior so that they are not exclusionary and can recognize the value of women's skills and contributions. As part of the new contract between partners, men have had to become more involved in child care and housework. Although the split is not 50/50 in most households, men are still doing more of this type of work at home than ever before (Douthitt, 1989; Jump & Haas, 1987). Some of the benefits of the dual-career marriage have been the extra income that is earned when both partners work and the higher level of self-esteem in many women who are being paid for their work (Barnett & Baruch, 1987).

Like women, men are struggling with balancing work and home life (Gilbert, 1988). The corporate work ethic still expects its employees to put in extra hours to get the job done (Keen, 1991). The man who sacrifices time at the office for child care and family life runs the risk of stagnating in his career. As women have discovered, it is hard to be both a fast-track worker and an involved parent. Something must give. More men are deciding that their identity as a man can include being a good father, loving partner, and house cleaner. The need to prove yourself in the work environment can now be tempered with these other roles for a more balanced masculinity.

Mick, a 35-year-old husband and father in a dual-career marriage, still experiences conflict between his work and home life.

> I want to be a good dad and caring partner, but sometimes my work requires me to stay late at the office. My superiors don't want to hear excuses about how my kid was sick or I promised to take my daughter to her dance recital. A few years ago that would have bothered me. Now I feel like my family comes first. I do a good enough job but I'm probably not the rising superstar I thought I was going to be. There is some loss of identity with my work, I guess, but I can live with that. I feel like my priorities are straight now.

EPILOGUE

As might be expected, I fell into the hard worker camp on my summer jobs as a young man. Now, however, I have been questioning more and more the ultimate meaning of work for me. I have noticed it has really changed over the last several years, as the theories suggest it might. Before I had a child, it was easy to make commitments to my job. To get ahead, I'd put in extra hours and often bring work home to do in the evenings or on weekends. I was praised by my superiors and respected by my peers as being a high-achieving colleague. When I reached the top level in my job, I was faced with the prospect of continuing to work extra time with no tangible reward except a pat on the back. It crossed my mind to change positions and move to another town where I might be paid better and given more responsibility. On the other hand, I had established myself in the community and knew that moving would mean starting over. Instead of putting in extra time at work, I began to find hobbies like wine tasting and started running during my lunch break. Suddenly, life opened up its possibilities. When my daughter arrived, my spouse and I really had to restructure our lives to make time for her because we were both working. Now I'm busy again, but it's not so much work that is calling on me; rather, it is home life that I am struggling to find time for. ∎

SUMMARY

Work has been one of the most important ways a man expresses his identity. Although work roles are less gender specific than in the past, a good number of men still feel conflict when they share the breadwinner role in the family. When making career choices, many males are handicapped in their decision making by learned gender role stereotypes about what jobs men and women are supposed to do. Even so, some men are choosing nontraditional careers as they follow their interests, values, and abilities. Social scientists who study work find that at each stage of life men must negotiate different passages in relation to their vocational choice. No longer is it expected that a man hold the same job throughout his whole life. Finding a balance between a healthy work identity and a full life outside of work is a challenge with which many men continue to struggle.

CONSCIOUSNESS-RAISING ACTIVITIES
ACTIVITY 1

Think of the messages you received as you grew up about work and the value of work in your life. These messages might have come from parents, teachers, magazines, or organizations (for example, the Boy Scouts). Some examples of these messages might be "A man must work hard" or "It's not OK to miss work, even when you don't feel well." Write down ten socialization messages you received.

MESSAGE   AGREE/DISAGREE

1. _____   _____

2. _____   _____

3. _____   _____

4. _____   _____

5. _____   _____

6. _____   _____

7. _____   _____

8. _____   _____

9. _____   _____

10. _____   _____

Now go back through your list and, next to each message you listed, indicate whether you agree or disagree with it. What does this list tell you about the way our culture influences men and how they feel about work? How do you feel about these messages?

ACTIVITY 2

View several popular evening television shows, such as "L.A. Law," "Evening Shade," "Doogie Howser, M.D.," or "Matlock." Focus on the male characters. Write down their names, the shows on which they appear, their occupations, and one or two of their characteristics. Do they appear happy in their work? Do they talk about their work to the other characters? What message do these programs give men about the value of their careers?

PERSONAL DEVELOPMENT EXERCISES
EXERCISE 1
Think for a moment and write down five career fantasies you can recall from your own childhood.

1. _____

2. _____

3. _____

4. _____

5. _____

What do you think about these fantasies? Do they seem to accurately reflect you as you know yourself today? How typical, or how unusual, do you think they are? Were they influenced by important role models? Who were the models? How do these fantasies, or the models upon whom they are based, continue to play a part in your life today?

EXERCISE 2
To explore some of the early influences on your career choice, let's now focus on the values your parents held about work. Consider each parent and imagine interviewing them about work. Write down two things each would say about work if you were to ask them "What messages or values about work did you hope to convey to your children?"

Mother: 1. _____

2. _____

Father: 1. _____

2. _____

How do these messages fit with your values about work? Would you tell your children anything different?

EXERCISE 3
Consider each of the following satisfactions people derive from work. Rate the importance each one would play in your own choice of an occupation or career using the following scale:

1 = not important at all
2 = somewhat important
3 = reasonably important
4 = very important

_____ Help society

_____ Help others

_____ Make public contact

_____ Work with other people

_____ Be competitive

_____ Make decisions

_____ Work under pressure

_____ Have power and authority

_____ Make large amounts of money

_____ Work in a desirable location

_____ Have a lot of variety

_____ Influence people

_____ Work alone

_____ Gain knowledge

_____ Be creative

_____ Supervise others

_____ Have job stability

_____ Be recognized

_____ Be independent

_____ Be famous

Look over your responses and notice those that were most and least important. How do these work satisfactions fit with your current job or your planned career? What might be the obstacles to getting all of your career satisfactions met? How might you decide on what is most important to you?

REFERENCES

Barnett, R. C., & Baruch, G. K. (1987). Social roles, gender, and psychological distress. In R. C. Barnett, L. Biener, & G. K. Baruch (Eds.), *Gender and stress* (pp. 122–143). New York: Free Press.

Berglass, S. (1986). *The success syndrome: Hitting bottom when you reach the top.* New York: Plenum Press.

Bernard, J. (1981). The good provider role: Its rise and fall. *American Psychologist, 36,* 1–12.

Bridges, J. S. (1989). Sex differences in occupational values. *Sex Roles, 20,* 205–211.

Castaneda, C. (1968). *The teachings of Don Juan.* Berkeley and Los Angeles: University of California Press.

Cowan, C. P., & Bronstein, P. (1988). Father's roles in the family: Implications for research, intervention and change. In P. Bronstein & C. P. Cowan (Eds.),

Fatherhood today: Men's changing role in the family (pp. 341–348). New York: Wiley.

CRITES, J. O., & FITZGERALD, L. F. (1978). The competent male. *The Counseling Psychologist, 7,* 10–14.

DAVID, D. S., & BRANNON, R. (Eds.). (1976). *The forty-nine percent majority: The male sex role.* Reading, MA: Addison-Wesley.

DOUTHITT, R. A. (1989). The division of labor within the home: Have gender roles changed? *Sex Roles, 20,* 693–704.

DOYLE, J. A. (1989). *The male experience.* Dubuque, IA: William C. Brown.

EITZEN, D. S. (1975). Athletes in the status system of male adolescents: A replication of Coleman's *The adolescent society. Adolescence, 10,* 268–276.

ERIKSON, E. (1982). *The life cycle completed.* New York: Bantam Books.

FASSEL, D. (1990). *Working ourselves to death: The high costs of workaholism and the rewards of recovery.* San Francisco: HarperCollins.

FASTEAU, M. (1974). *The male machine.* New York: McGraw-Hill.

FIELDS, R., TAYLOR, P., WEYLER, R., & INGRASCI, R. (1984). *Chop wood carry water.* Los Angeles: Tarcher.

FILLENBAUM, C. G., GEORGE, L. K., & PALMORE, E. G. (1985). Determinants and consequences of retirement among men of different races and economic levels. *Journal of Gerontology, 40,* 85–94.

FINE, G. A. (1987). One of the boys: Women in male-dominated settings. In M. S. Kimmel (Ed.), *Changing men* (pp. 131–147). Newbury Park, CA: Sage.

FREUDENBERG, H. J., & RICHELSON, G. (1980). *Burnout: The high cost of achievement.* New York: Bantam Books.

GERZON, M. (1982). *A choice of heroes.* Boston: Houghton Mifflin.

GILBERT, L. A. (1987). Women and men together but equal: Issues for men in dual career marriages. In M. Scher, M. Stevens, G. Good, & G. A. Eichenfield (Eds.), *Handbook of counseling and psychotherapy with men* (pp. 278–293). Newbury Park, CA: Sage.

GILBERT, L. A. (1988). *Sharing it all: The rewards and struggles of two-career families.* New York: Plenum Press.

GINZBERG, E. (1972). Toward a theory of occupational choice: A restatement. *Vocational Guidance Quarterly, 20,* 169–176.

GOULD, R. E. (1974). Measuring masculinity by the size of a paycheck. In J. H. Pleck & J. Sawyer (Eds.), *Men and masculinity* (pp. 96–100). Englewood Cliffs, NJ: Prentice-Hall.

GOULD, R. L. (1978). *Transformations: Growth and change in adult life.* New York: Simon & Schuster.

HARRISON, J. (1978). Warning: The male sex role may be dangerous to your health. *Journal of Social Issues, 34,* 65–85.

HOLLAND, J. (1966). *The psychology of vocational choice.* Waltham, MA: Blaisdell.

HOLLAND, J. (1985). *Making vocational choices: A theory of vocational personalities and work environments* (2nd ed.). Englewood Cliffs, NJ: Prentice-Hall.

JUMP, T. L., & HAAS, L. (1987). Fathers in transition: Dual-career fathers participating in child care. In M. S. Kimmel (Ed.), *Changing men* (pp. 98–114). Newbury Park, CA: Sage.

KEEN, S. (1991). *Fire in the belly: On being a man.* New York: Bantam Books.

KOHN, A. (1986). *No contest: The case against competition.* Boston: Houghton Mifflin.

LEVINSON, D., DARROW, C., KLEIN, E., LEVINSON, M., & McKEE, B. (1978). *The seasons of a man's life.* New York: Knopf.

MESSNER, M. (1987). The life of a man's seasons: Male identity in the life course of the jock. In M. S. Kimmel (Ed.), *Changing men* (pp. 37–52). Newbury Park, CA: Sage.

MESSNER, M. A. (1992). Boyhood, organized sports, and the construction of masculinities. In M. S. Kimmel & M. A. Messner (Eds.), *Men's lives* (pp. 161–176). New York: Macmillan.

NAISBITT, J. (1984). *Megatrends.* New York: Warner.

O'NEIL, J. M., & FISHMAN, D. (1986). Adult men's career transitions and gender role themes. In Z. B. Leibowitz & H. D. Lea (Eds.), *Adult career development: Concepts, issues, and practices* (pp. 132–162). Alexandria, VA: National Career Development Association.

PARHAM, T. A., & McDAVIS, R. J. (1987). Black men, an endangered species: Who's really pulling the trigger? *Journal of Counseling and Development, 66,* 24–27.

PARNES, H. (1981). *Work and retirement: A longitudinal study of men.* Cambridge, MA: MIT Press.

PLECK, J. H. (1975). The male sex role: Definitions, problems, and sources of change. *Journal of Social Issues, 32,* 155–164.

PLECK, J. H. (1985). *Working wives/working husbands.* Newbury Park, CA: Sage.

ROE, A., & LUNNEBORG, P. W. (1990). Personality development and career choice. In D. Brown, L. Brooks, & Associates, *Career choice and development: Applying contemporary theories to practice* (pp. 68–101). San Francisco: Jossey-Bass.

ROSS, C. E., & HUBER, J. (1985). Hardship and depression. *Journal of Health and Social Behavior, 26,* 312–327.

SKOVHOLT, T. M. (1990). Career themes in counseling and psychotherapy with men. In D. Moore & F. Leafgren (Eds.), *Men in conflict* (pp. 39–56). Alexandria, VA: American Association for Counseling and Development.

SKOVHOLT, T. M., & MORGAN, J. I. (1981). Career development: An outline of issues for men. *Personnel and Guidance Journal, 60,* 231–237.

STANWORTH, M. (1983). *Gender and schooling: A study of sexual divisions in the classroom*. London: Hutchinson.

SUPER, D. (1984). Career and life development. In D. Brown, L. Brooks, & Associates, *Career choice and development: Applying contemporary theories to practice*. San Francisco: Jossey-Bass.

SUPER, D. (1990). A life span, life space approach to career development. In D. Brown, L. Brooks, & Associates, *Career choice and development: Applying contemporary theories to practice* (2nd ed., pp. 197–261). San Francisco: Jossey-Bass.

TERKEL, S. (1975). *Working*. New York: Avon.

TIEDEMAN, D. V., & O'HARA, R. P. (1963). *Career development: Choice and adjustment*. New York: College Entrance Examination Board.

WEGMANN, R., CHAPMAN, R., & JOHNSON, M. (1989). *Work in the new economy*. Alexandria, VA: American Association of Counseling and Development.

WEISS, R. S. (1990). *Staying the course: The emotional and social lives of men who do well at work*. New York: Free Press.

SUGGESTED READINGS

BOLLES, R. (1981). *The three boxes of life*. Berkeley, CA: Ten Speed Press.

BROWN, D., BROOKS, L., & ASSOCIATES. (1990). *Career choice and development* (2nd ed.). San Francisco: Jossey-Bass.

GILBERT, L. A. (1985). *Men in dual-career families: Current realities and future prospects*. Hillsdale, NJ: Erlbaum.

GOULD, R. L. (1978). *Transformations: Growth and change in adult life*. New York: Simon & Schuster.

HILLS, S. M. (Ed.). (1986). *The changing labor market: A longitudinal study of young men*. Lexington, MA: Lexington Books.

KOHN, A. (1986). *No contest: The case against competition*. Boston: Houghton Mifflin.

LEVINSON, D. J., DARROW, C. N., KLEIN, E. B., LEVINSON, M. H., & McKEE, B. (1978). *The seasons of a man's life*. New York: Knopf.

SMELSER, N. J., & ERIKSON, E. H. (Eds.). (1980). *Themes of work and love in adulthood*. Cambridge, MA: Harvard University Press.

TERKEL, S. (1975). *Working*. New York: Avon Books.

VALLIANT, G. E. (1977). *Adaptation to life*. Boston: Little, Brown.

WEISS, R. S. (1990). *Staying the course: The emotional and social lives of men who do well at work*. New York: Free Press.

CHAPTER 7

A MAN'S HEALTH

PROLOGUE

A young boy's first encounter with human mortality is bound to change forever the way he views himself and others who matter to him. I remember when the idea of death and the fear of losing a loved one was brought home to me. I was six years old, playing in the living room on a warm August afternoon. I was engaged in overseeing a war I was having between my toy soldiers. For some reason, I felt an urgency for my father to be there playing with me. I searched for him, wandering around our small house, looking from room to room. All was quiet. Finally, I found him lying down in his bedroom in the back of the house. With one arm over his forehead, he lay motionless in the dark, still room. Having never seen my dad looking so passive and weak, I was immediately frightened. Sensing danger, I softly asked him, "Dad, what's wrong?" Slowly, he turned his head to look at me and said, "Sammy, I have a bad headache and I need to take a little nap." Sensing my discomfort, he added, "Don't worry, I'll be all right." Even with this verbal affirmation, I had the strong feeling that he wasn't telling me the whole truth. A shudder of aloneness swept through my body and something deep in me was changed forever. Although I couldn't verbalize these thoughts, for the first time I knew my father to be less than the infallible protector he had always been to me. His lapse into sickness awakened me to his vulnerability. I realized he would not live forever. ∎

INTRODUCTION: THE HEALTH MYTH

If asked what associations they would make between the words *men* and *health,* most people might conjure images of sleek, tanned, virile young bodies pumping iron. They might further visualize someone who resembles a hybrid of the Marlboro Man and Arnold Schwarzenegger. They might think the healthy man is never ill, always in shape, strong, silent, determined, and invulnerable. Of course, this is not surprising since these are the images promoted through advertising, media, and popular heroes. Indeed, these images are so pervasive one has only to pick up a current magazine that is geared to the young adult male segment of the market and thumb through it to get some idea of the messages men are given regarding what it means to be a man, to be healthy and in good shape.

These messages, and the images contained in them, are much more fantasy than fact. They are overtly designed to sell a product, and covertly they perpetuate and reinforce a number of gender-role stereotypes. As we begin to probe beneath these glossy full-color images into the reality of male health, we find a more complicated situation.

When we look more carefully at men's health issues, we find some that are disconcerting and others that are deeply disturbing. A man's life expectancy is in general between seven and eight years less than a woman's in Western, industrialized countries (Stillion, 1985). Men are much more likely to die in motor vehicle and work-related accidents than women (Waldron & Johnson, 1976). They are three times as likely to commit suicide and five times as likely to die from homicide as their female counterparts (Harrison, 1978). More men die from ailments that are widely considered to be preventable, such as pulmonary heart disease, cirrhosis of the liver, emphysema, as well as cancers of the digestive system and repiratory system (Harrison, 1978). In addition, men are more likely to exhibit problems with alcohol and illicit drug abuse (Meinecke, 1981) and less likely to consult medical or mental health services for health-related assistance (Good, Dell, & Mintz, 1989). The images portrayed in our popular media obviously are not the whole picture.

THE CAUSES OF MEN'S HEALTH PROBLEMS

Researchers disagree about the reasons for the greater number of male health problems. Some researchers favor a more biological explanation; others endorse a more psychosocial explanation (Madigan, 1957; Retherford, 1975). Those in the biological camp have suggested that beginning as early as conception, males are predisposed to be biologically disadvantaged. The Y chromosome that distinguishes the genetic male from the female is smaller and carries less genetic material than the X chromosome, of which women have two and men only one. There are more than 60 diseases to which men are more susceptible that are linked to the Y chromosome (Montagu,

1974). Males are conceived at a ratio of 120:100 compared with females. However, higher spontaneous abortion rates of male fetuses lowers this ratio to 106:100 at birth. It is thought that the male fetus is more vulnerable to intrauterine problems than the female fetus during pregancy (Harrison, 1978). Even though more males are born, the higher mortality rate of males after birth makes them a minority by the age of 30. Most researchers and theorists who believe that psychosocial factors are most important in men's health problems readily admit that there is likely to be a predisoposed biological advantage for women. However, environmental, social, and psychological factors are thought to exacerbate the problems for men (Goldberg, 1976; Harrison, 1978; Meinecke, 1981).

Environmental circumstances such as military service, work settings, and possession of firearms directly impact male mortality rates. Many more men than women have been injured and killed in military-related activity and from working in high-risk environments, such as construction sites, farms, factories, and mines (Doyle, 1989). In the United States, where gun control laws are lax, more men than women die as a result of gunshot wounds, sometimes self-inflicted (Kellerman & Reay, 1986). Clearly, when men put themselves in more dangerous circumstances, they run a heightened risk to their health. Compounding this problem has been the tendency for men not to seek health care except when in acute crisis (Good, Dell, & Mintz, 1989; Harris & Guten, 1979). The old saying, "If it ain't broke, don't fix it" seems to describe men's approach to their health.

Those who believe that social and psychological factors play an important role in men's health have identified the male gender role as the culprit (Goldberg, 1976, 1979; Harrison, 1978; O'Neil, 1981). Socialized since childhood to live up to the expectations of the masculine ideal, many men have literally killed themselves in its pursuit. By defining ourselves by our toughness, stoicism, competitiveness, and power, we are left with little room to accept our needs for affection, love, and care. These are considered weaknesses associated with femininity that must be avoided at all costs (Brannon, 1976; O'Neil, 1981). To compensate for these supposed failings, many men engage in hypermasculine behaviors that are often dangerous and self-destructive (Meinecke, 1981). These include acts of aggression and violence, excessive alcohol and drug consumption, and high-risk behaviors, such as driving too fast or engaging in promiscuous sex (Harrison, 1978). A result of the hypermasculine behavior is a disregard for one's own body that may eventually lead to both short-term and long-term health problems.

Associated with the masculine ideal is the highly competitive, achievement oriented stance to which many men aspire. The socialized need to be in control and in power makes many men ignore their bodies and emotional needs in the service of accomplishment (O'Neil, 1981). Type A behavior, characterized by an aggressive and unyielding desire to accomplish goals at all costs, has been indicted as a major contributor to coronary heart disease in men (Friedman & Rosenman, 1974). Individuals who exhibit this pattern of behavior often have a poor diet, ignore physical health symptoms, and are known to engage in compulsive smoking, eating, or caffeine consumption. Research has shown that heavy users of caffeine, in combination with cigarettes and alcohol, are at high risk for a variety of progressive diseases as well as poorer psychological functioning (James & Crosbie, 1987). Because they deny their need for human contact and nurturance, those showing Type A behaviors often receive very little social support from others. Social support has been shown to be a significant factor in reducing health-related problems and speeding recovery from disease (Gentry & Kobasa, 1984; Reynolds & Kaplan, 1990; Vaillant & Vaillant, 1990).

Denial of that which is feminine has been implicated as a major component of the male gender-role ideal (O'Neil, 1981). Asking for help, expressing feelings, admitting weakness, and acknowledging health concerns are behaviors traditional men avoid. Unlike most women, when a man recognizes that he is sick or doesn't feel right, he is faced with a dilemma. To admit to feeling bad runs against his illusion of physical invulnerability. To deny the feeling means to live in pain and distress. Too often men opt to minimize their distress in order to carry on with their work or activity. The result can mean a worsening physical condition, psychological distress in the form of depression and anxiety, a weakened immune system, or a susceptibility to other health-related disorders (Goldberg, 1979; Selye, 1956).

Chuck, a 47-year-old man in remission from cancer, admits that he ignored many of the warning signs of stress in his life.

> I never missed a day of work until I was diagnosed with my illness. There were days when I felt sick or had a terrible headache, but I prided myself on being at work sick or not. I had no patience with my employees who complained or who missed work. I never realized what impact my denial had until I got the cancer. Now I wish that I had paid attention to the signals my body was giving me. Today I am sensitive to what my body tells me. I rest when I need to and have no qualms about missing some work. I want to live.

Alcohol and drug abuse have been other ways some men harm themselves physically and emotionally. Because the traditional male role provides few outlets for emotional expression, many men keep their feelings bottled up inside. A visit to the local tavern or lodge after work has traditionally provided men with male camaraderie and a place to release frustration (Thompson, 1986). Unfortunately, alcohol and tobacco products have often accompanied these rituals, leading to increases in aggressive behavior as well as to long-term substance abuse patterns among those who are vulnerable (Diamond, 1987). For instance, men who batter their spouses and children are more likely to have abused alcohol (Sonkin, Martin, & Walker, 1985). It appears that males who use alcohol and drugs to cope with stress create a spiraling pattern of addiction in which the substances eventually disrupt their lives more than the original problems from which they were seeking escape (Cooper, Russell, & George, 1988). Contrast these realities to the idealized media images of men in bars drinking in the company of beautiful women.

Oliver, a 35-year-old man who has abstained from drugs and alcohol for the past seven years, describes his experience:

> I have a problem with drugs and alcohol. Every day I struggle with my addiction even though I haven't indulged in several years. I used to party and get myself into wild situations in which I would put myself in physical danger or end up hurting someone else. I was indiscriminate in my sexual behavior. I was just pure crazy when I was using. I have been through a rehab program and go to A.A. meetings every day. It's been my salvation to feel the support of others struggling with the same issues. Today I have a pretty normal life. I think I am a good father and husband, and my business has been quite successful.

Traditional masculine values toward sexuality have also become hazardous to a man's health. It is not unusual in dormitories or fraternity houses to hear men talk about women with whom they have slept. Even though most men exaggerate, there is an ethos that one should try to "score" as much as possible (Gross, 1978). Sexual conquest has been the ultimate masculine rite of passage for many men (Keen, 1991). While evidence suggests that most men usually keep their sexual desires in check, under the influence of drugs and alcohol, sexual inhibitions are greatly decreased (Masters, Johnson, & Kolodny, 1988). During these times men and women are most susceptible to engaging in unprotected sex, creating the possibility of dangerous consequences to themselves and others. Not only do men risk contracting sexually transmitted diseases such as the AIDS virus through unprotected promiscuous behavior, they also risk impregnating their partners or being accused of rape or sexual assault if they have forced themselves on a person who didn't have the same desire for sexual contact.

WELLNESS: A RESPONSE TO SELF-DESTRUCTION

Health used to be defined as the absence of sickness. The current definition of health advanced by the World Health Organization (1958) suggests that health is a state of positive well-being and not merely the absence of disease. In this country, an interest in a more holistic approach to wellness continues to develop. This approach has promoted a comprehensive, personal orientation to developing and maintaining good mental, physical, and spiritual health. The basis for this approach is self-awareness and personal responsibility (Travis & Ryan, 1981). The individual's inner capacity for health is acknowledged and used to develop positive health habits. Most current evaluations of an individual's health emphasize personal values, goals, aspirations, and self-identified strengths as well as areas for positive growth. Health is not merely a set of laboratory findings that are within normal limits. Rather it involves the whole person in developing and maintaining a positive and health-promoting life-style that leads to a personal and subjective sense of satisfaction and well-being (Meinecke, 1981).

Men have a special stake in adopting a life-style based on wellness rather than on self-destruction. Even though the male gender role promotes behavior that is often unhealthy, most men want to live a long life that is fulfilling and satisfying. To function optimally, it is important for a man to assess the various aspects of his life and how well he is maintaining his health. The National Wellness Institute suggests that each man look at six overlapping wellness dimensions: physical, emotional, social, occupational, intellectual, and spiritual (Leafgren, 1990).

PHYSICAL WELLNESS

Even though a man's body is his temple, many of us treat our bodies poorly. Some of the abuse of our bodies comes from events over which we had no control. Trying to conform to the demands of a male role that denies the feminine aspects of ourselves has left many of us not only inhibited from expressing ourselves emotionally, but also rigid in our bodies. Character armor, the physical manifestation of the denial of emotional expression, may show up as a tightened jaw, a stiff neck and back, shallow, restricted breathing, a rigid pelvic area, an inability to cry, being over- or underweight, and a number of other chronic body aches (Lowen, 1975). Recent studies suggest that men as well as women have negative perceptions of their own body size and weight (McCaulay, Mintz, & Glenn, 1988). Many men compare themselves negatively to muscular body-builder types, and experience lower self-esteem.

Men can reclaim their bodies through nutrition, exercise, giving up drugs and alcohol, practicing relaxation, and through body-oriented therapies. As a start, men need to make sure that they are eating properly. Diet is one of the strongest contributors to the body's health. Eating regular, balanced meals that give the body sufficient quantities of protein, carbohydrates, fats, and necessary vitamins gives us a head start in coping with stress. Nutritionists have linked the ingestion of certain foods with various mood states (Davis, 1985). It is important that each of us take note of how we feel on our current diet and make changes that fit our own body functioning.

Another significant means of keeping our body functioning is through exercise. Many men find that as their work and family obligations become more pressing, exercise is one of the first activities to be eliminated. Aside from the endorphin high that occurs with a vigorous workout, many men find that they are calmer and less prone to agitation and angry outbursts when they have exercised. Exercise often releases pent-up frustration and pressures. Brian, a 55-year-old college administrator, runs daily to keep his job manageable. "I am challenged every day by my job. There are always people who wanted me to respond yesterday to their demands today. If I didn't run every day at lunch, I would have quit this job by now."

The body also demands that we have sufficient sleep to function at our fullest capacity. Although this isn't always possible, getting a minimum of seven hours of sleep a night greatly reduces mistakes and misperceptions in work and relationships. In addition, those who sleep less tend to use artificial stimulants to keep them alert, such as caffeine and nicotine, which have long-term destructive effects on the body (James & Crosbie, 1987). Depressant-type drugs used to relieve anxiety and promote sleep, such as alcohol, barbiturates, and sedatives, can become addictive and life threatening. It is important that men learn to rely less on drugs to alter their moods and more on coping skills that allow us to feel our natural emotions and experience life fully.

Practicing relaxation through meditation, sitting quietly just letting your mind wander, taking nature walks, or listening to music without interuption are some of the ways men can tune back in to their bodies. These events will not happen on their own but rather must be planned into your day. The demands of work, school, friends, or family will need to wait as you take 10, 20, or 30 minutes to relax and get back in touch with yourself.

For men who have chronic muscle tension, treating yourself to a professional massage or visiting a chiropractor or body worker might be a good self-care choice. When muscular tension has its roots in childhood emotional or physical abuse, an appointment with a qualified mental health practitioner who uses body work might be in order.

EMOTIONAL WELLNESS

The admonition "big boys don't cry" speaks for itself. A growing boy's emotional life is frequently shunted aside by our culture's emphasis on activity and accomplishment. Emotions are often denied, avoided, and discredited (O'Neil, 1981). From an early age, little boys are taught not to cry by subtle, and sometimes not so subtle, experiences. They are belittled and shamed both by their peers and by well-intentioned adults. Encouraged to solve problems independently and work things out on their own, many boys grow up to be men who have learned to deny and hold in their emotions.

Challenging the male gender role prohibition of feeling is the task of the man who wants wellness in this dimension of his life. Acknowledging your own emotions and being prepared to face your hidden emotions is not an easy step to take. To do this, a man must be prepared to experience feelings he has purposely denied for fear of being shamed or seen as weak. He must slow down what he is doing and pay attention to the subtle body signals that speak to him throughout his day. A man must listen and respect what the signals tell him, whether it be "I'm tired," "I'm mad," "I'm lost," or "I'm hurt."

Living an emotionally rich life may mean moving away from using logic as the sole means of making decisions about what to do in certain situations. Men who are emotionally free use their feelings to guide them through difficult dilemmas. Reason and logic have their places in the construction of impersonal objects and events, but often our emotional lives are not understood this way. While our emotions do work systematically, rarely are we able to decipher their meaning without taking into account a number of variables of which our rational mind can barely keep track.

Men often need help with the emotional part of themselves, and this runs against the traditional male role of being self-sufficient (Brannon, 1976). Men need to be in relationships with other men and women who are in touch with their emotional selves. It is important for us to feel safe and to trust so we can risk being irrational, emotional, and even silly. We need to learn to trust ourselves enough to find new outlets and activities that go beyond our old limited repetoire of behaviors. Some men might benefit from individual or group therapy that encourages emotional expression in a safe and private setting. You can learn to feel free emotionally with patience, determination, and a desire for self-discovery.

SOCIAL WELLNESS

The insistence in our culture that men solve their problems alone causes shame and self-loathing in those who are faced with dilemmas that are insoluble without help. One of the negative effects of this rugged individualism is that many men carry their burden with them, wearing down vulnerable body organs and isolating themselves with their silence from other people (Gerzon, 1982; Goldberg, 1979).

The solution for the isolated man is to make friendship and camaraderie a priority in his life (Letich, 1991). As men leave institutional settings such as high school or college, there are less built-in opportunities to maintain relationships. Men who involve themselves in community projects and extracurricular activities can actively seek out the company of other men and women who have similar interests. Making an effort to be intimate with family members through honest sharing and listening is also a way to reduce feelings of loneliness and isolation. Research demonstrates that individuals with strong support networks have better mental health and a higher recovery rate from illness and loss (Gentry & Kobasa, 1984; Reynolds & Kaplan, 1990; Vaillant & Vaillant, 1990).

For men who have experienced trauma or a lifelong pattern of isolation, meeting with a counselor or psychotherapist might be an important first step in finding ways to break out from self-containment. All-male groups may also benefit men who find it easier to relate to women than to other men.

OCCUPATIONAL WELLNESS

Work is the arena in which men seem to define themselves most comfortably. However, the work environment is often not conducive to a healthy life-style. Environmental hazards such as toxic chemicals in a factory setting or working in dangerous places on a construction job can make occupational safety difficult to attain. The competition between coworkers or rival companies can make the work environment stressful and emotionally demanding. Many men arrive at home tired at the end of a work day with little energy for other activities or relationships. Some men do jobs that don't excite or interest them in order to get a paycheck. They pay for this disinterest with boredom and a loss of meaning that may result in depression and susceptibility to substance abuse.

In order to improve the occupational dimension of his life, a man must first determine his motivation and interest in the work he is doing. He owes it to himself to visit a career development center if he is unhappy with his work to find out what type of career best matches his interests, values, and abilities. If the job is right but the work environment is poor, then it is a man's responsibility to try to make changes by talking to superiors or coworkers about improving the situation. If this isn't possible, maybe it means switching companies or going into business for yourself.

In highly competitive situations, it may be important for a man to practice stress management strategies to lighten his burden. For instance, exercising at lunchtime, taking meditation breaks during the day, eating well, and being assertive about your limits may make a demanding job more manageable. Men can also work to improve communication with their coworkers, superiors, and employees as a way to reduce interpersonal conflicts on the job. Often being able to listen, reflect, and suggest solutions is better than grumbling to yourself or talking behind another person's back.

Sometimes a man needs new career challenges, especially if he has been working at the same job for many years. Asking for new work responsibilities, a new position, or a special project may give him a renewed sense of purpose on the job. Other men have been known to switch careers altogether, learning new skills and perspectives that are stimulating and renewing. Taking the risk to change the status quo is every man's responsibility if he is bored or unhappy with his job. Occupational satisfaction is an essential component in a man's quest for a healthy life.

INTELLECTUAL WELLNESS

The intellectual dimension of a man's life is often lost in his lack of time for activity outside of his work and family life. Compared to women, men are notorious for being nonreaders of material outside of the sports page of the newspaper or work-related information. Perhaps the television age has made watching a movie or TV show easier at the end of a hard day than opening a novel. Having an intellectual challenge in your life that requires extensive use of cognitive skills to figure out a problem or create a new situation is a healthy, stimulating process.

Intellectual wellness may also refer to having interests in the world outside of yourself. It may mean getting involved in the community, politics, the environment, or trying to understand poetry. Traveling, attending cultural events such as plays and concerts, and involving yourself in painting, writing, reading, or learning a musical instrument are ways you can stimulate yourself to think in a creative and more global fashion. Enrolling in a class on a subject that interests you or taking a course in a subject area of which you have no knowledge is a structured way to be intellectually stimulated. Since it is a common male characteristic to become involved in intellectual pursuits to avoiding emotions or relationships, the intellectual dimension should not become so dominating that other aspects of your wellness are sacrificed.

SPIRITUAL WELLNESS

Closely related to the intellectual dimension of wellness is the spiritual realm. Spirituality refers to man's yearning for a deeper connection with life's meaning and truth. Although many of us are raised with spiritual values through our families and religious upbringing, each man develops his own philosophy of life that fits his experience. A man must have some purpose for living if he is to thrive (Frankl, 1963). Men who lose their purpose are prime candidates for substance abuse, depression, and suicide (Yalom, 1980). It is not uncommon for a man who has relied solely on his work for purpose to become depressed and despondent when he loses his job or must face retirement.

It is important for us to develop a picture or theme of our lives that incorporates our relationships, work, beliefs, values, and experiences. To have some sense of a power greater than ourselves lets us bond with other humans in kinship. The mysterious wonders of life, of our species, planet, and universe are our common link to all the generations of people who have come before us and will come after us. Astronauts who have seen the earth from outer space have marveled at the magnificence of our planet and have been moved to reflect on their contribution to the history of humankind. For some men, having children provides them with a higher purpose, knowing that a part of them will continue to live on past their death. For others, writing a book or creating a work of art that will transcend their own lives gives them a sense of meaning and purpose.

While there is no one path to spiritual awareness and enlightenment, we must give ourselves the time to ponder and reflect about our existence. For some men, this might happen in church. For others it may be through taking a hike in the mountains or fishing in a favorite lake or stream. Whatever your way, it is important to consider your place in the universe in order to give perspective and meaning to your life.

BEING A CONSCIOUS CONSUMER OF HEALTH CARE

Traditional approaches to health, health care, and health maintenance draw heavily on the role of the physician as the expert who we visit when we are ailing, and who will, with a flick of the wrist, write a prescription or excise an offending tissue. There is little acknowledgment, much less active support, for a consciousness of health maintenance and illness prevention. The doctor knows it all, and we need only consult him or her when we have an obvious need. Implicit in such an approach is a passive, compliant, and uneducated role for the patient (Taylor, 1986).

Fortunately, this approach is rapidly giving way to one that promotes the responsibility each man has for care and maintenance of his body, mind, and spirit. This preventive or wellness approach emphasizes self-knowledge, self-care, and self-responsibility. The individual becomes an active participant in the maintenance of his health, educates himself about his body, mind, and spirit, and actively works to prevent illness and disease.

Little boys can learn both positive and negative health habits by observing valued adult male role models.

When a need arises for consultation with a health-care professional, such a person is knowledgeable and educated about his problems and about the kinds of care available. He becomes an active consumer in securing health care for himself (Pelletier, 1979).

The two approaches are far from mutually exclusive. However, the wellness approach has much to offer individuals who want to assume responsibility for their own health and to work to prevent unnecessary health-care expenses as well as unwanted illness. While the wellness approach might be difficult for many men to adopt who have been socialized to minimize health concerns, the emphasis on taking responsibility for their health might be attractive to men who have had to face breakdowns in their physical and psychological functioning.

MAKING A HEALTH CHANGE PLAN

It is often a signal from the body that motivates many men to make health changes. The inability to keep up physically because of being overweight, coughing and repeated respiratory ailments from smoking, or a warning from a physician about high blood pressure are common motivators for health improvement.

If you are ready to make wellness a part of your life, remember that it is important not to try to change everything at once. Small, clear, specific goals are easier to achieve than large, general, or vague goals. Before you begin the change, monitor the behaviors that are causing you distress so that you can notice the difference once you have begun to work on the new behavior. It is important to offer yourself rewards for the new behavior and to have the support of another person while you are making the changes in your life-style. You might consult health professionals who have special information on nutrition, physiology, and exercise. Failures are likely to occur since none of us are perfect. It will serve you best to accept that you might relapse. It took a long time to develop a bad habit, and it will take some time to change it. What is significant is to learn from any setbacks you experience as you get back on track. Finally, if you want to change, you must be able to imagine the positive benefits of the behavior change to maintain your motivation.

Allen, a 29-year-old man who has been working to change his life-style habits, shares the wellness plan he created for himself.

> I am 5 feet 8 inches tall and used to weigh over 250 pounds. I loved junk food and ate whenever my hands weren't busy. Of course, I

hated my body, but I was unmotivated to change. It wasn't until I was told by my physician that I had developed diabetes and that my cholesterol level placed me in danger of having an early heart attack that I decided to do something about my weight and the way I lived my life. My initial goals were to drop 75 pounds, to eat healthy foods, and to exercise regularly. I visited a nutritionist who helped me put together a low-fat diet. I cleared out my apartment of all food and restocked it with food for my diet. I rewarded myself for staying on the diet by having one meal out a week at a restaurant where I could have anything I wanted within reason. I also joined a support group called Overeater's Anonymous that let me see that I wasn't alone with the problem. I met some good people who I learned to trust with some of my darkest secrets. They supported me when I got down on myself for relapsing in my diet plan on two different occasions. I also joined a health club that I still go to five days a week. I worked out a fitness plan with one of their counselors that involved weights, swimming, and stationary bike riding. After two years on my plan, I now weigh 165 pounds and feel great. I'm always surprised when I see myself in the mirror because I still perceive myself as a fat person. An added benefit to this plan is that I have begun dating, something I totally avoided before. My newest health goals are to learn some new sports like wind surfing or tennis that will let me be outside more. I have also begun to see a counselor to help me look at some of the causes of my obesity and to help me have more confidence in my relationships.

EPILOGUE

Now that I have a daughter, I am even more aware of the things that might go wrong in life. I want to live as long as I can so I can see her grow up and live her life. I know that if I don't take care of myself, I am only cheating myself. That has motivated me to get involved with long-distance running and being much more careful with what I eat. I used to eat rich food that was high in fat. When my doctor showed me the results of my physical, I vowed to change my diet. While I still love rich food, I only eat it on special occasions these days. I try not to overwork, I make special time to spend with my wife and daughter, and I also try to take some time during the day to be alone with myself. In recent years, as I have begun to reflect more upon the meaning of life, I have found myself attending church and really enjoying the fellowship and shared awe in our existence. I'm hoping that the changes I have made in my life will have a positive impact on my daughter as I serve as one of her role models.

SUMMARY

Despite the media's presentation of young, attractive, muscle-bound men, most males have tended to ignore their health needs in the pursuit of achievement-oriented activities or because of their ignorance about the relationship between mind and body. Statistics point to glaring problems in men's health compared to women's health, including a higher suicide rate and shorter life expectancy. The wellness approach that involves men in becoming aware of the physical, emotional, social, occupational, intellectual, and spiritual dimensions of their lives can counteract the destructiveness of many male gender-role behaviors. Men are encouraged to take charge of their health to prevent distress and breakdown instead of relying on a disease approach that treats the person only when he is sick or diseased. A healthy man will approach his health care in a way that emphasizes self-awareness, attention to emotional stressors, and self-responsibility. By pursuing goals he has created from a self-assessment of the various dimensions of his life, he is more likely to live with vigor, purpose, and well-being.

CONSCIOUSNESS-RAISING ACTIVITIES
ACTIVITY 1

Collect a few current magazines that are geared toward men. Some examples are *Men's Fitness, GQ, Men's Health,* and *Sports Illustrated.* Sit down with a pencil and paper and start at the beginning of one of these magazines. Look at each page; evaluate and categorize the male models under some of the following headings:

Race—African-American, white, Asian, Latino or Hispanic
Physical condition—able-bodied, blind, wheelchair-bound
Age—young, middle-aged, old, white-haired, wrinkled
Other—physique, attractiveness, and so on

Reflect on what kind of messages this advertising sends to men in our society about health.

Now make a list of the articles that relate to men's health issues in the magazines. Categorize them according to content. Evaluate whether they promote wellness, health maintenance, and disease prevention. What conclusions can be drawn about the effect of these kinds of media articles?

ACTIVITY 2

With a partner, develop a list of the ways that the two of you and others you know respond to stress. Divide the list into healthy ways to respond to stress and unhealthy ways. For instance, you might list meditation on the healthy list and smoking cigarettes on the unhealthy list. In addition, notice any gender differences in the ways that each sex copes with stress. When you have completed your lists, compare them with others in the class or group.

PERSONAL DEVELOPMENT EXERCISES
EXERCISE 1

A wellness approach to your health begins with self-awareness and a careful self-assessment of the following physical, emotional, and spiritual domains of one's life. Carefully consider your own level of wellness in each of these areas.

SLEEP
Do you fall asleep easily at night?
Do you usually sleep soundly through the night?
Do you wake up rested and alert each morning?

EATING HABITS
Do you eat from the four basic food groups each meal?
Do you include variety in your meals?
Do you eat breakfast each morning?
Do you limit your intake of fat, salt, and refined sugar?

SAFETY HABITS
Do you use a shoulder-seat belt in your car?
Do you drive defensively and obey all traffic laws?

Are you careful when working around your house or apartment?
Do you read instructions carefully and avoid careless mistakes?

Exercise and Fitness Habits
Do you attempt to maintain a reasonable weight?
Do you engage in vigorous exercise three times a week?

Personal Health Habits
Do you keep your body clean on a daily basis?
Do you floss and brush your teeth on a daily basis?
If not circumsized, do you clean under your foreskin regularly?
Do you check your testes for unusual lumps or growths regularly?
If appropriate, do you have your prostate gland checked?

Substance Use
Do you exercise moderation in your use of alcohol?
Do you avoid using mood-altering chemicals to manage stress?
Do you follow directions when using prescription drugs?

Emotional and Spiritual Habits
Do you try to solve your problems as they arise?
Do you look forward to the future with optimism?
Do you practice spiritual values that give meaning to your life?
Do you feel happy, content, and secure?

EXERCISE 2

An important element in a wholistic or wellness approach to life is a clear understanding of your health values. Think about each of the following ten health values, and rank them in order from 1 to 10, with 1 representing the most important; 10, the least important.

RANK

_____ To maintain a healthy diet.

_____ To exercise at least three times a week.

_____ To participate in a religious service or community of some kind on a regular basis.

_____ To have happy, satisfying interpersonal relationships.

_____ To have a body I am proud of.

_____ To be able to solve my problems on my own as they come up.

_____ To maintain a healthy, appropriate weight.

_____ To get regular medical and dental checkups.

_____ To engage in a satisfying career.

_____ To have a happy and satisfying family life.

Now consider your rankings. Is there anything you might want to change in your life in light of these rankings? How do you feel about what you ranked high and low?

EXERCISE 3

On the basis of what you have read and learned in this chapter, think of one personal health-related goal for yourself. A goal is best stated in concrete, achievable, and realistic terms. For example, to start an exercise program within the next week, or to lose ten pounds before the next holiday season, or to stop smoking cigarettes. Plan a goal for yourself and tell another person about it. Then make a commitment to check back with them in a period of time to tell them how you are progressing.

REFERENCES

BRANNON, R. (1976). The male sex role: Our culture's blueprint for manhood and what it's done for us lately. In D. David & R. Brannon (Eds.), *The forty-nine percent majority: The male sex role* (pp. 1–45). Reading, MA: Addison-Wesley.

COOPER, M. L., RUSSELL, M., & GEORGE, W. H. (1988). Coping, expectancies, and alcohol abuse: A test of social learning formulations. *Journal of Abnormal Psychology, 97,* 218–230.

DAVIS, A. (1985). *Let's stay healthy: A guide to lifelong nutrition.* New York: New American Library.

DIAMOND, J. (1987). Counseling male substance abusers. In M. Scher, M. Stevens, G. Good, & G. A. Eichenfield (Eds.), *Handbook of counseling and psychotherapy with men* (pp. 332–342). Newbury Park, CA: Sage.

DOYLE, J. A. (1989). *The male experience.* Dubuque, IA: William C. Brown.

FRANKL, V. (1963). *Man's search for meaning.* New York: Washington Square Press.

FRIEDMAN, M., & ROSENMAN, R. H. (1974). *Type A behavior and your heart.* New York: Knopf.

GENTRY, W. D., & KOBASA, S. C. (1984). Social and psychological resources mediating stress-illness relationships in humans. In W. D. Gentry (Ed.), *Handbook of behavioural medicine* (pp. 87–116). New York: Guilford Press.

GERZON, M. (1982). *A choice of heroes*. Boston: Houghton Mifflin.

GOLDBERG, H. (1976). *The hazards of being male*. New York: Signet.

GOLDBERG, H. (1979). *The new male: From self-destruction to self-care*. New York: Morrow.

GOOD, G., DELL, D. M., & MINTZ, L. B. (1989). Male roles and gender conflict: Relationships to help-seeking in men. *Journal of Counseling Psychology, 3,* 295–300.

GROSS, A. E. (1978). The male sex role and heterosexual behavior. *Journal of Social Issues, 34,* 87–107.

HARRIS, D. M., & GUTEN, S. (1979). Health protective behavior: An exploratory study. *Journal of Health and Social Behavior, 20,* 17–29.

HARRISON, J. (1978). Warning: The male sex role may be dangerous to your health. *Journal of Social Issues, 34,* 65–86.

JAMES, J. E., & CROSBIE, J. (1987). Somatic and psychological health implications of heavy caffeine use. *British Journal of Addiction, 82,* 503–509.

KEEN, S. (1991). *Fire in the belly: On being a man*. New York: Bantam Books.

KELLERMAN, A., & REAY, D. (1986). Protection or peril? An analysis of firearm-related deaths in the home. *New England Journal of Medicine, 314,* 1557–1560.

LEAFGREN, F. (1990). Being a man can be hazardous to your health: Lifestyle issues. In D. Moore & F. Leafgren (Eds.), *Men in conflict* (pp. 265–276). Alexandria, VA: American Association for Counseling and Development.

LETICH, L. (1991). Do you know who your friends are? *Utne Reader, 45,* 85–87.

LOWEN, A. (1975). Bioenergetics. New York: Penguin Books.

MADIGAN, F. (1957). Are sex mortality differentials biologically caused? *Millbank Memorial Fund Quarterly, 35,* 202–223.

MASTERS, W. H., JOHNSON, V. E., & KOLODNY, R. C. (1988). *Human sexuality*. Glenview, IL: Scott, Foresman.

MCCAULEY, M., MINTZ, L., & GLENN, A. A. (1988). Body image, self-esteem, and depression-proneness: Closing the gender gap. *Sex Roles, 18,* 381–391.

MEINECKE, C. E. (1981). Socialized to die younger? Hypermasculinity and men's health. *Personnel and Guidance Journal, 60,* 241–245.

MONTAGU, A. (1974). *The natural superiority of women*. New York: Collier.

O'NEIL, J. M. (1981). Patterns of gender role conflict and strain: Sexism and fear of femininity in men's lives. *Personnel and Guidance Journal, 60,* 203–210.

PELLETIER, K. R. (1979). *Holistic medicine*. New York: Delacorte.

RETHERFORD, R. (1975). *The changing sex differential in mortality*. Westport, CT: Greenwood.

REYNOLDS, P., & KAPLAN, G. A. (1990). Social connections and risk for cancer: Prospective evidence from the Alameda County study. *Behavioral-Medicine, 16,* 101–110.

SELYE, H. (1956). *The stress of life.* New York: McGraw-Hill.

SONKIN, D., MARTIN, D., & WALKER, L. (1985). *The male batterer: A treatment approach.* New York: Springer.

STILLION, J. (1985). *Death and the sexes: An examination of differential longevity, attitudes, behaviors, and coping skills.* New York: Hemisphere.

TAYLOR, S. E. (1986). *Health psychology.* New York: Random House.

THOMPSON, K. (1986). A man needs a lodge. *Utne Reader, 15,* 49–53.

TRAVIS, J. W., & RYAN, S. R. (1981). *The wellness workbook.* Berkeley, CA: Ten Speed Press.

VAILLANT, G. E., & VAILLANT, C. O. (1990). Natural history of male psychological health: XII. *American Journal of Psychiatry, 147,* 31–37.

WALDRON, I., & JOHNSON, S. (1976). Why do women live longer than men? *Journal of Human Stress, 2,* 19–29.

WORLD HEALTH ORGANIZATION. (1958). *Expert committee on health education of the public* (Technical Report Series No. 89). Geneva, Switzerland: Author.

YALOM, I. D. (1980). *Existential psychotherapy.* New York: Basic Books.

SUGGESTED READINGS

BLISS, S. (Ed.). (1991). *The new holistic health handbook: Living well in a new age.* Lexington, MA: Stephen Greene Press.

BLOOMFIELD, H. A., & KORY, R. B. (1980). *The wholistic way to health and happiness.* New York: Simon & Schuster.

COOPER, R. K. (1989). *Health and fitness excellence.* Boston: Houghton Mifflin.

DAVIS, A. (1985). *Let's stay healthy: A guide to lifelong nutrition.* New York: New American Library.

EMETH, E. V., & GREENHUT, J. H. (1991). *The wholeness handbook: Care of body, mind, and spirit for optimal health.* New York: Continuum.

FRANKL, V. (1963). *Man's search for meaning.* New York: Washington Square Press.

GOLDBERG, H. (1976). *The hazards of being male.* New York: Signet.

O'NEIL, J. M. (1981). Patterns of gender role conflict and strain: Sexism and fear of femininity in men's lives. *Personnel and Guidance Journal, 60,* 203–210.

SELYE, H. (1956). *The stress of life.* New York: McGraw-Hill.

TRAVIS, J. W., & RYAN, R. S. (1981). *Wellness workbook.* Berkeley, CA: Ten Speed Press.

UNIVERSITY OF CALIFORNIA, BERKELEY. (1991). *The wellness encyclopedia: The comprehensive family resource for safeguarding health and preventing illness.* Boston: Houghton Mifflin.

WITKIN-LANOIL, G. (1986). *The male stress syndrome.* New York: Newmarker Press.

CHAPTER 8

STAYING ALIVE:
EMBRACING
THE MALE SPIRIT

PROLOGUE

"This can't be happening to me!" I cried out in my empty bedroom. My relationship with the woman I had loved for the past seven years was coming to an end. She had been staying out late without explanation, and I was hurting like never before. At times, I was extremely angry, but mostly I felt sorry for myself, to the point of contemplating self-destruction. I was such a good guy. I didn't deserve this. Secretly, I had always been afraid of this happening since I had gotten involved with her. I was scared to death of being abandoned, left alone, and not having another person there to give my life some direction and meaning.

In the next several months, my feelings of wanting to reverse what happened gradually changed to acknowledging that I was really alone and that I was actually surviving. I was getting support from friends and finding that I had a hidden reservoir of strength that was helping me stand on my own two feet. My wound was giving me a deeper perspective on life, including a realization that pain was an essential element in learning important life lessons about myself and others. Although I didn't feel capable of reentering an intense relationship, I found that I could still enjoy playful relationships with women. I grew closer to my male friends who I perceived could understand my feelings while not demanding too much from me.

A year after my breakup, I was ready to venture out on my own. Accompanied by my dog, I moved to the West Coast, excited to see the kind of life I would create for myself. Living alone without friends or family would be my real test of inner strength. Could I become my own best friend? Would I be able to learn the lessons of life without having someone to lean on for the easy answers?

I felt lonely. I struggled to find an identity in my work. But I also rediscovered my lost joy of painting. I traveled to various parts of the West, and I entered my own psychotherapy to explore more deeply the conflicts that had been unearthed by my emotional wounding. For the first time in my life, I began to enjoy my own company and didn't need others to lean on. Even though I still appreciated companionship, I wasn't desperate for it. ■

INTRODUCTION: THE SPIRITUAL JOURNEY

This book has outlined the many ways men have been bound by traditional male socialization. It has also described a number of alternative paths that men might choose to live a less restricted and more bountiful existence. The goal of questioning, challenging, and revising the traditional male values has been to create a more balanced and self-aware masculine identity. We simply cannot afford to go on arrogantly treating each other, women, or the planet as though we are always in command of the situation when we are not. The deconstruction of the traditional male role leaves us in unknown territory. Rather than retreat into more rigid behavior, we have an opportunity to explore and discover who we are, how we might improve our lives, and make our world a better place. This awareness puts us on a path of a spiritual nature, a journey that has the potential to give us new meaning and new perspectives in our lives. To free the male spirit from its bondage in shame and cultural constraints, we must transcend our familial and cultural upbringing.

This journey, which will take us from the familiar roles we learned in our family and culture to new and sometimes untested ways of being, will not be an easy one. Several authors have suggested that as a man leaves the familiar territory of his cultural upbringing he must be ready to face various challenges to his identity (Bly, 1990; Keen, 1991; Moore, Parker, Thompson, & Dougherty, 1990; Peck, 1980). Keen (1991) reminds us that the road that extends beyond what is known will expose us to our fears, our uncertainty, and our despair. But it will also offer us an opportunity to know ourselves better, feel closer in our interpersonal relationships, and be freed to give something back to our families, communities, and planet.

This chapter describes our interpretation of the nature of the male spirit and how it is lost, regained, and nourished. We are not advocating any one way to discover the spiritual self, but rather are offering ideas and resources that might stimulate you to pursue spirituality for yourself. Spirituality, for the purposes of this chapter, does not equate to being religious. We have used the term as a metaphor for living life with vigor, meaning, and compassion for humanity.

IDENTIFYING THE MALE SPIRITUAL SELF

Life constantly presents opportunities to grow and learn about yourself. Unfortunately, when we are trying to stay in control, in power, and in charge, we often ignore the subtle events that may be our teachers. We have been taught to be autonomous, independent, and self-contained. On the way to an important class or meeting, rehearsing what we are supposed to have learned or prepared, it is easy for us to miss the colors, smells, and sounds being encountered by our senses. Contrast this image with one of walking on the beach during a vacation when you are acutely aware of the smell of the ocean, birds flying overhead, and the wind blowing across your face. The former evokes feelings of anxiety about performance while the latter brings up a sense of appreciation for being alive, a part of the natural world.

One way to think about spirituality is to view it as man's yearning for a deeper connection with life's meaning and truth. It is our relationship to the wonders and mystery of life as we know it. It is our awareness of the special and sacred quality of our existence. The spiritual self is manifested in each of us as an integration of the instinctive, passionate animal and the thoughtful, empathic member of the human community. The passionate animal moves with grace through his environment, alert to his senses, and responsive with his body (Lowen, 1990). The empathic human readily feels his emotions, marvels in his thoughts, and directs his actions in a way that demonstrates compassion for his fellow creatures (Keen, 1991). He feels a part of the world and yet is aware of his aloneness. If you have ever seen a child openly encounter the world with his or her senses, you are witnessing the freely curious energy that drives our species to create, dream, and act.

While the male child captures this spiritual nature best through his playfulness and curiosity, he is discouraged by our culture from embracing it fully. As he gets older, the importance of getting things done, being productive, and acting like a responsible adult often stifles the male from reacquainting himself with the more spiritual part of himself. Often, it is a crisis or loss that compels men to rediscover their spirituality.

THE LITTLE BOY: GUIDING THE MALE SPIRIT

The little boy we would like to describe is a metaphor for the spiritual self that existed before our indoctrination into the adult world by family, school, and society. Like the inner child that Bradshaw (1990) and Whitfield (1987) discuss, the little boy is sensitive to others and himself and very clear about his needs for affection, warmth, and security. When he feels secure, the little boy can do whatever he wants without doubt, guilt, or shame. If he feels like playing in the dirt, he does so without thinking, "What if I get dirty and track mud in the house and make Mom mad?" The little boy is spontaneous in his actions and feels his emotions strongly. Whether thwarted by reality or thrown into situations he doesn't quite understand, the little boy has no problem expressing his fear, anger, and frustration or even his desire to be held, hugged, and cuddled without shame. The life of the little boy could be described as adventurous, warm, and emotionally rich.

What happens to that little boy as he grows up? The familiar scenario for most of us is that he encounters others who do not value or appreciate his spontaneity, honest feelings, or openness to the world. Rather than be accepted as he is, he is told, "Big boys don't cry!" "Don't be a sissy!" "Quit daydreaming and get in the game!" "Win!" He is made to feel shameful for acknowledging pain, showing fear, or wanting a hug. He is also reminded that a real man doesn't let his feelings show. Gradually, through extended contact with the traditional male world, the little boy in many of us becomes stifled, shamed, and finally buried so that we become anxious and distrustful of this aspect of ourselves.

Miller (1981) describes the mask or personality that develops to protect a person from shame and embarrassment as the false self. Many men wear this false self to shield themselves and others from the vulnerable and needy little boy whom they have hidden. With time, the false outer self is often mistaken for the real self and becomes the basis for a persona that is tough, unemotional, and inexpressive in the face of conflict or difficult circumstances (Osherson & Krugman, 1990; Scher, 1979).

Jimmy, an 8-year-old boy whose parents were recently divorced, denied that he was angry or disappointed when his Dad cancelled his weekend visit. Instead, he acted cool and aloof during their next visit together, not giving any indication to his father of his inner pain. Unfortunately, his father was unaware of the pain he had caused his son. Both of them felt awkward and emotionally disconnected, unable to touch the little boy in each other.

When the little boy inside is shut off from expression, spontaneous actions are often replaced by calculated behaviors designed to meet the demands of the culture. As the boy grows physically into a man, his continued lack of communication with his true self results in distorted reactions to others based on external social rules rather than inner conviction (Jourard, 1971). Because he is cut off from his inner little boy, he may be guided in his choice of a mate by superficial appearance rather than a deeper awareness of who would best be able to nurture the playful and expressive part of himself (Goldberg, 1983). Natural inclinations toward expressing love, taking emotional risks, and feeling compassion may be lost to the voices of authority figures and peer culture who dictate correct behavior. In order to cope with the uncomfortable discrepancy between the inner child's needs and the societal messages for perfection and emotional denial, many men distract themselves through life-styles based on competition, addiction, and self-righteousness (Goldberg, 1979).

THE LOSS OF THE MALE SPIRIT

If we have become cut off from the inner self, we have lost our most valuable means of making intuitive sense of our world. Relying on society's definitions and rules about masculinity rather than their own often leaves men feeling empty or vaguely aware of anxiety, guilt, and shame at some point in their lives (Keen, 1991). Even though men have been taught to be logical and analytical in their reactions to events in the world, the events themselves are hardly rational. We often feel weak, impotent, and helpless in responding because we are not in control of what is happening. As little boys, we were able to let go, cry, and get a hug when the world got crazy. But as adult men we are expected to cope silently by trying to control what is happening (Brannon, 1976). Trying to control an uncontrollable world is a tiring task and usually a losing battle. If we give in to our sadness, hopelessness, or frustration, we feel anxious and ashamed because of what we learned growing up. It is not all right to cry or express our pain, so we have to find other, less vulnerable outlets for our feelings.

The work ethic, with its promises of wealth and fame, provides an acceptable outlet for pent-up energy. Working late into the night on a project with a deadline gives a man the feeling that what he is doing is important and that he will be rewarded for his mastery. He is fulfilling his impulse toward autonomy (Gaylin, 1992). His success will be defined by winning, an emotional high impervious to others' attempts to shame him. If he is successful enough, he will be untouchable and yet desirable to members of the opposite sex, he believes (Farrell, 1986). His inner little boy will be protected from pain by a big house, a fancy car, a beautiful mate, and the ability to outmaneuver the other male competitors. If only this fantasy were true.

Robert, a 55-year-old successful businessman in a men's group, reveals otherwise:

> I worked so hard to make sure that I would never need anyone. I built several successful businesses, made as much money as I could have dreamed of having, married a beautiful woman, but I couldn't protect myself from being hurt. My wife left me, I was betrayed by an associate, and I only feel the pain I was trying to escape more intensely.

Many men have forgotten how to make contact with the inner spiritual self even when they want this part to emerge. Some stumble into a cycle of addiction. This leads them to compulsively repeat a pleasurable behavior that only mimics the spiritual high they are missing. Although these behaviors, such as alcohol and drug addiction or compulsive sex, are initially pleasurable, addictions tend to take on exaggerated importance and pull the individual away from the freedom and spontaneity that he originally may have sought (Carnes, 1988). Most men have to learn from the unavoidable pain they experience in life how to recapture the spiritual self that was once theirs (Peck, 1980).

RECAPTURING THE MALE SPIRIT

Many men do not realize that they have been dead to the inner self until a tragedy, such as the loss of a loved one, reminds them of their mortality and vulnerability. These painful events are openings into the deeper aspects of self. The anger and grief that he feels in his body fundamentally changes the way a man looks at his life. It will be hard for him to maintain his arrogant, detached, or logical stance; he becomes fearful of what lurks buried beneath the socially molded outer layer of his personality. Robert Bly (1990), a poet and leader in the mythopoetic men's movement, speaks of a "descent into the ashes" that each man must follow to truly discover his spiritual self.

The descent is not easy. It is fraught with stored images of shameful experiences that have long been submerged into the unconscious. Accompanying these images are socially unacceptable emotional states including fear, rage, and depression. Bly (1990) suggests that men need to experience their grief over having had to inhibit so much of their true nature. It is an incredible awakening when a man realizes that he has created his life based on the expectations and reinforcements of others, rather than on what internally moves him. He feels incredibly frightened and sad about the numbing choices he has made in his life without the guidance of a more spiritually grounded self.

Our society has rarely provided ways for men to learn from their pain. Typically men are given a grace period to temporarily feel sadness after a loss, but then they are expected to return to society without being fundamentally changed by the experience. For instance, the soldiers who fought in Vietnam were not only given little understanding or compassion upon returning home, but actually shamed by our society (Gerzon, 1982). The deep wounding that occurred in the jungle killing fields had to be buried. The result was severe cultural and psychological maladjustment for many returning veterns (Kaylor, King, & King, 1987).

If men are to reclaim their spiritual selves, they need to have the time, space, and support of other men. The profeminist men's movement beginning in the 1970s and the mythopoetic and psychotherapeutic men's movements of the 1980s and early 1990s have acknowledged the importance

Isolation can be avoided by pursuing friendships with other men.

of men gathering together to tell their stories, feel their pain, and celebrate the inner self that has been repressed (Clatterbaugh, 1990). Permission has been given during men's groups and retreats to speak of the terror, confusion, rape, grief, and shame that men have had to silence in order to be socially acceptable. It is not unusual to find that as these strong feelings are released, compassion, empathy, and love emerge in men who can't remember the last time they cried (Adler, Springen, Glick, & Gordon, 1991).

THE NATURE OF THE INNER MASCULINE SPIRITUAL JOURNEY

Traditionally, men in our culture have passed through developmental milestones that have impacted their lives at various stages (Erikson, 1980; Gould, 1978; Levinson et al., 1978; Vaillant, 1977). From birth to death a man is faced with challenges to his identity, from taking his first steps to going to school, finding a job, pursuing a mate, having a family, retirement, and facing his own mortality. How a man encounters and makes sense of these milestones will determine the satisfaction he derives from his life and the meaning he gives it. All men face the challenge of these external events, but few use these passages to explore their feelings and fantasies, and to interpret these events. Most men will accept the passive way, respond as they were taught by family and culture, and spend little time reflecting on the meaning of what has happened to them.

It is only recently that men have begun to see their lives in a more mythic fashion (Keen, 1991; Keen & Valley-Fox, 1989; Moore & Gillette, 1990). Rather than conceptualize our existence by the external events only, these authors suggest that we ponder the meaning of events and act as heroes in the unfolding drama of our lives. The implication of this approach is that all life encounters are important learning situations if we choose to view them that way. We can look back at events in our lives that we didn't see at the time as significant, and derive meaning and perspective from them. For instance, many of us have taken our relationships with our parents for granted because our parents were already here when we arrived in the world. By looking back at the nature of those relationships and events that occurred, a man can begin to understand how these important people affected his life. As an adult, a man can more clearly see his parents as human beings with foibles rather than the godlike protectors they were to him as a child.

The authors who describe the inner male journey use metaphors and images to depict the process (Bly, 1990). Historically, men have had little awareness and even less vocabulary to capture the nature of their inner world. Images from the outer world applied to inner psychological states seem to resonate well with many men in their quest for self-understanding. Freud (1949) and Jung (1967) are the pioneers of exploring this inner world through dream symbols, free association, and intensive self-reflection. We will take you through a sampling of the images, symbols, and psychological events that men can use to make sense of their inner lives. It is important to remember that the sequence may vary from man to man and that the symbols do not mean the same thing to every man. In fact, each of us must struggle with a host of possible meanings to find those significant to us personally.

The earliest event that deserves reflection is the birth of the infant. Moving from the dark, liquid protection of the womb to the lighted expanse of our world has been described as the birth trauma (Rank, 1964). It is literally the first and perhaps most intense psychological passage we encounter. Even though most of us do not remember this event, it has impacted all of us. Men who have difficulty with starting new projects or making decisions to head in a new direction with life might use the image of being born to help them understand the fears and loss of control that come with moving into unknown territory.

The loss of the female bond with mother has been described as a very significant event for most men (Bowlby, 1988; Osherson, 1986). Having bonded with the mother or female caretaker, the little boy eventually begins to locomote away from her as he matures. Chodorow (1978) suggests that he must sever his ties with his mother, cutting the bond in order to identify with his father or male caretaker and enter the world of men. Many men who have difficulty with intimate relations with women might pause to imagine the emotional pain that they might have been feeling as they moved away from their mothers. Keen (1991) warns that many men have not worked out conflicted feelings they have about their mothers; the result is some strange compensating behaviors toward women. A man might superimpose the image of the all-encompassing mother on a potential mate. Such a man may then distance himself emotionally for fear of being engulfed by her or try to dominate to keep her from being too dangerous.

The means by which men are initiated into manhood have received much attention in recent years (Bly, 1990; Keen, 1991). Eliade (1975) and Gilmore (1990) describe various initiation experiences for boys of different cultures. What they have in common is a separation from the parents, a visit to unknown territory such as the woods or wilderness, and a wounding of the boy by the male elders of the group. The wounding, which might be a scratching with a knife or whipping with tree branches, is meant not to be sadistic abuse but rather a marker that the boy will remember as a part of his initiation into manhood. Religious Jews use the Bar Mitzvah at age 13 as a male initiation rite in which the boy leads the congregation in prayers and reads from the Torah, an event for which he prepares for more than a year (Brod, 1988).

Bly (1986) has suggested that the way most men in our culture are initiated is diffuse and informal. Getting a driver's license, going to a rock concert, becoming drunk or high, getting one's first job, or having sex for the first time rarely involve the elders of the tribe welcoming a boy into manhood. The popularity of men's retreats in which masks are made, fires are lit, and drums are beaten can be traced to the desire of some men to have a ritual initiation experience into manhood. The absence of this event in men's lives clouds the passage from adolescence to adulthood and discourages a connection between men from different generations.

The loss of a parent or loved one is one of the most powerful events in a man's life. The grief felt is real and reflects our ultimate aloneness in the world. While one's parents are alive, it is comforting to know that you can still call on those who raised you. Even if they are old and you are smarter, parents sometimes possess wisdom from their life journey that can be soothing and provide security. When a parent dies, the omnipotence of your own life crumbles (Gould, 1978). You can never retrieve your parents except in your memory. Many men, unaware of the psychological impact of this event, carry on in their everyday life. Without open grieving, which men in our culture have difficulty expressing, unconscious processes take over (Freud, 1974). Some men experience an uncomfortableness with their lives that manifests itself in changing partners or a low-grade depression, while others lose their optimism and begin to feel despair (Bly, 1990).

Loss (not necessarily death), whether it be of a parent, mate, or partner, can give a man a window into deeper aspects of himself. Despair may allow him to reevaluate his life goals, remind him of his aloneness and mortality, and provide him with a clearer sense of the cyclical nature of life. Ultimately, a man who has support and coping resources can emerge from a period of grief with renewed energy and the awareness that he is all right just the way he is. Because he accepts himself, he has no need to prove himself over and over again (Keen, 1991).

GETTING HELP WITH THE JOURNEY

Because the inner male spiritual journey is often frightening to encounter alone, a man who wants to bring deeper understanding and meaning into his life is encouraged to have assistance. There are a variety of perspectives and approaches to wrestling with the issues, conflicts, and feelings that arise from living life with awareness. Each man is unique. You may find that one or more approaches best matches your style and way of understanding.

INDIVIDUAL COUNSELING AND PSYCHOTHERAPY

While many men have perceived counseling and psychotherapy as admitting weakness or incompetence, the reality is that this process works to slowly take down the walls of the outer mask, allowing you to explore the internal aspects of yourself. Individual therapy has the advantage of letting you go at your own pace in a relationship with a therapist that is built on trust and confidentiality. While many men feel more comfortable with a female therapist because of the cultural role that allows us to more readily admit our feelings to women, it might be important to work out our male conflicts with a male therapist. The types of issues that arise in therapy include feelings of inadequacy in work, conflicts about intimacy, strained relationships with fathers and mothers, concern about addictive behaviors, fears about expressing deeper feelings, generalized life anxiety, and finding meaning in life. Regardless of the type of method the therapist uses, it is essential that you find a therapist you like and respect; otherwise you might not open up in an honest way. For further descriptions on approaches to therapy, refer to Corey and Corey (1990) and Yalom (1980).

THERAPEUTIC MEN'S GROUP WORK

Although men gathering in groups is not a new phenomenon, there is a significant difference in the quality of personal sharing when men gather as part of a therapeutic group. All-male group therapy has been useful for men recovering from addictions, for veterans of war experiences, and more recently for men who are wanting to challenge themselves to be open and honest with who they are in the presence of fellow males. Rather than see other men as competitors, the focus in such a group tends to be on emotional support and bonding. Challenging interpersonal blocks, reliving shameful experiences, and learning to allow the inner self freedom of expression are some of the potential benefits. Typically, therapeutic groups are led by a trained psychotherapist who is able to intervene to facilitate the expression of emotion and help direct interpersonal dialogues. For further reading on group interventions, see Rabinowitz and Cochran (1987), Stein (1983), and Yalom (1975).

RECOVERY GROUP WORK

Recovery group work usually involves men trying to overcome addictions to drugs and alcohol or cope with the effects of exposure to dysfunctional or abusive family patterns. While not as interpersonally oriented as the therapeutic groups, the focus is on self-revelation in the presence of others who have gone through similar pain. There is an emphasis on sharing one's shame and gaining support from the group for releasing hidden secrets. Many of these groups, such as those focused on codependency, emphasize discovering the child within and understanding family dynamics as a pathway to wholeness. Others, such as Alcoholics or Narcotics Anonymous, believe in contacting your higher power as a means to recovery. These groups are often led by recovering members who know firsthand the dangers of denial and self-destruction. Recovery groups are often used as an adjunct to individual therapy and may be a part of followup treatment from an inpatient addiction program. Often, members of the family are included in separate groups as a way for a man in recovery to confront painful family secrets and find new ways to relate to family. For further reading on this perspective see Bradshaw (1988, 1990) and Weiss and Weiss (1989).

MYTHOPOETIC MEN'S RITUALS AND ACTIVITIES

The mythopoetic men's movement has recently gained popularity in North America. Influenced by writer Robert Bly and Jungian psychologists and mythologists, this movement uses storytelling, reinterpretation of myths and fairy tales, and ritual ceremonies to help men reacquaint themselves with the masculine and feminine aspects of themselves. In a large-group or retreat format men gather for up to several days away from the mainstream culture to talk, dance, listen to stories, and create symbols of their inner sense of masculinity. Believing that men in the modern age no longer have rites of passage into manhood, the mythopoetic leaders have designed experiences based on the ancestral rituals of past cultures to give men a strong sense of initiation by other men. Elder men are encouraged to nourish and guide younger men emotionally. Some of the activities that allow men to let go of their cultural shells and go deeper into themselves include drumming, dancing, mask making, martial arts, guided imagery, singing, game playing, story telling, body work, dream analysis, and sharing personal feelings as they arise. The all-male format encourages men to rebalance their masculine and feminine selves and to reenter society with greater compassion and emotional energy. For further information on this approach, see Bly (1990), Liebman (1991), and Moyers and Bly (1990).

Body Work

Body work involves the use of touch to heal painful emotional wounds. Believing that the mind and body are intimately connected, practitioners of body work manipulate muscles and encourage body movement and relaxation to uncover stored emotional trauma. Alexander Lowen, the founder of Bioenergetic Analysis, believes that this method quickly breaks through the very rigid defenses of personality and leads to increased self-awareness. While not all practitioners who work with the body focus on freeing the inner self, a less rigid and more relaxed body does leave one more open to doing inner exploration. Body work, combined with other therapeutic processes, is a powerful means of gaining access to the spiritual self. For further information on body work, see Kurtz (1990) and Lowen (1975, 1990).

Reading

Reading is an important means to stimulate thinking about what it means to be a man. Many men read only the sports page or material required for work or school. A trip to the library or bookstore will be enlightening as you realize that much has been written about understanding the male experience from a variety of perspectives. Books on self-improvement, spirituality, male-female relationships, finding meaning in life, recovering from loss, father-son relationships, and the like may stimulate you to take actions that are more congruent with your inner desires.

Aspiring to a New Ideal

In our ordinary day-to-day routine it is difficult to pay attention to that which makes living an extraordinary experience. It is usually during odd moments, when a man isn't able to follow his usual routine, that he is most open to noticing beauty, grace, and the magical quality of life. If all is going as planned, we don't get the chance to get off the "highway" of life to see what is occuring on the "back roads." Men are especially tied to efficiency and routine as a means of keeping life controllable and productive. Taking time to be away from the daily details of life may provide a valuable opportunity for us to see what route we are taking.

We have suggested that men try to live up to a higher ideal. We have encouraged you to become aware of your feelings, attitudes, and behaviors so you can be more conscious of your actions and live with clearer intention. You have been asked to explore the relationship you had with your parents so you can choose to be an even better parent. The problems associated with male intimacy have been exposed, leaving you with the possibility of improving your relationships with other men and women. The male myths of sexual behavior have been outlined so you can better share your enjoyment of sexuality with your partner. The extreme importance of a man's work to his identity has been questioned so that you can choose how you want to be defined in the world of work. You have been warned about the health hazards of the traditional male role so you can remember to take good care of your physical and psychological health. Finally, you have been reminded to step back and notice your existence with wonder and amazement so you can find purpose and meaning in your life.

Most men rarely live up to the higher ideal. Those who are supposed to be our heroes, who we see on television and in movies, hardly ever say what they are feeling in their hearts. The man who has journeyed past his familial and cultural roots will probably not be spectacular or daring enough to play for television. He will have no need to be validated by an appearance on television or to preach his path as the only way to enlightenment. He will be a new kind of hero who listens to his friends with empathy. He will acknowledge his fear and doubt but take action he believes is right. He will take walks in nature and fight to preserve its beauty. The new hero will appreciate his aloneness and value his family and friends. He will be a good father not only to his children but to all children who cross his path. He will be gentle but not afraid to stand up for what he believes in. His work will give him fulfillment and give something back to people. He will take time for contemplation and learn to accept himself as he is, with his strengths and flaws.

EPILOGUE

As I look back on the period of aloneness in my life, I smile. My descent into the ashes allowed me to examine who I was and how I was living my life, and to touch the pain I had been denying. I emerged from my grief with a renewed appreciation for life and a sense of adventure. I created a life-style that allowed me to be on my own, to do what I wanted without having to check with someone else, and to get close to friends who became like family. I reacquainted myself with hobbies, set off on adventures, and learned to enjoy my own company. On one of my trips, I met the woman whom I would eventually marry. Unlike my other long-term relationship, which had its origins in my insecurity, this one was built on the belief that I am worth being loved and that I have the capacity to love. I haven't fretted about her abandoning me, since I know that I have the inner strength to take care of myself no matter what happens. While loving someone with all my heart runs the risk of causing pain, I know I can survive the inevitable wounds that life inflicts and learn from them as important lessons. ■

SUMMARY

In order to feel healthy and alive, you must rediscover your inner spiritual self that has been buried by the culture's emphasis on productivity, competition, and control. A sense of inner deadness, generalized anxiety, and loss of meaning may be signs that the spirit is waning. It is usually through a painful experience such as a loss or emotional wounding that many men are open and motivated to descend into themselves to find what makes them feel alive. A variety of approaches can help you with your inner spiritual journey. It is important to choose an approach that fits your style and way of understanding. You are encouraged to transcend your familial and cultural roles and to aspire to a higher masculine ideal as you live your life.

CONSCIOUSNESS-RAISING ACTIVITIES
ACTIVITY 1

Allow the class or group to engage in a ceremony honoring masculinity. Bring drums or percussion instruments to play. Have everyone form a circle in which each person is to share an aspect of their masculinity they are ashamed of and one that they are proud of. Other exercises might involve a naming ceremony where each person moves to the center of the circle and says his name, while the rest of the group listens and then repeats his name several times. This is a very powerful affirmation of being.

ACTIVITY 2

Each class or group member should bring an object or piece of art or writing of personal significance to share with the group. Taking turns, each member can reveal what is meaningful about this possession and in the process share a part of his inner self. This exercise works best when the class or group has built a sense of trust with one another. Often this exercise brings emotions to the surface so there will need to be sufficient time for all members to share and process the experience.

PERSONAL DEVELOPMENT EXERCISES
EXERCISE 1

Shut your eyes and try to visualize your inner little boy. If you have a picture of you as a little boy, find it and imagine yourself at the age depicted in the picture. If not, allow your imagination to take you back to when you were this age. What image, if any, do you have of your little boy? Describe him using several adjectives. What wisdom can the little boy share with you about how you are currently leading your life?

EXERCISE 2

Use the following scale to respond:

5 = This statement is true most of the time.
4 = This statement is true much of the time.
3 = This statement is true some of the time.
2 = This statement is occasionally true.
1 = This statement is true almost none of the time.

_____ I often feel like a phony in social situations.

_____ I am playful in my interactions with others.

_____ I often wonder what my purpose in life is supposed to be.

_____ I feel like I have had to take on many adult responsibilities.

_____ I feel inhibited when I am around a new group of people.

_____ It is easy for me to trust other men.

_____ I feel comfortable feeling my sadness and grief.

_____ I love to watch children play.

_____ I wish there were a ritual rite of passage into adulthood.

_____ I often feel excited and energized by my life.

Go over your answers and explain your ratings. Use these questions as a stimulus for writing about your own spiritual journey.

EXERCISE 3

Use the following questions as the basis for writing about spirituality in your life.

> How would you define *spirituality*?
> How do you feel toward the spiritual part of yourself?
> At what times does the spiritual self seem to emerge in your life?
> What would make it easier for you to be more spiritually open in your life?

REFERENCES

ADLER, J., SPRINGER, K., GLICK, D., & GORDON, J. (1991, June 24). Drums, sweat and tears. *Newsweek,* pp. 46–51.

BLY, R. (1986). Men's initiation rites. *Utne Reader, 15,* 42–49.

BLY, R. (1990). *Iron John: A book about men.* New York: Addison-Wesley.

BOWLBY, J. (1988). *A secure base: Parent-child attachment and healthy human development.* New York: Basic Books.

BRADSHAW, J. (1988). *Bradshaw on the family.* Deerfield Beach, FL: Health Communications.

BRADSHAW, J. (1990). *Homecoming: Reclaiming and championing your inner child.* New York: Bantam Books.

BRANNON, R. (1976). The male sex role: Our culture's blueprint for manhood, and what it's done for us lately. In D. David & R. Brannon (Eds.), *The forty-nine percent majority: The male sex role* (pp. 1–45). Reading, MA: Addison-Wesley.

BROD, H. (1988). *A mensch among men: Explorations in Jewish masculinity.* Freedom, CA: Crossing Press.

CARNES, P. (1988). *Contrary to love.* Irvine, CA: Compcare.

CHODOROW, N. (1978). *The reproduction of mothering.* Berkeley and Los Angeles: University of California Press.

CLATTERBAUGH, K. (1990). *Contemporary perspectives on masculinity.* Boulder, CO: Westview.

COREY, G., & COREY, M. (1990). *Theory and practice of counseling and psychotherapy.* Pacific Grove, CA: Brooks/Cole.

ELIADE, M. (1975). *Rites and symbols of initiation.* New York: Harper & Row.

ERIKSON, E. H. (1980). *Identity and the life cycle.* New York: Norton.

FARRELL, W. (1986). *Why men are the way they are.* New York: McGraw-Hill.

FREUD, S. (1949). *An outline of psychoanalysis* (J. Strachey, Trans.). New York: Norton.

FREUD, S. (1974). Mourning and melancholia. In J. Strachey (Trans.), *Standard edition of the complete works of Sigmund Freud* (Vol. 14). London: Hogarth Press.

GAYLIN, W. (1992). *The male ego.* New York: Viking.

GERZON, M. (1982). *A choice of heroes.* Boston: Houghton Mifflin.

GILMORE, D. D. (1990). *Manhood in the making.* New Haven, CT: Yale University Press.

GOLDBERG, H. (1979). *The new male: From self destruction to self care.* New York: Morrow.

GOLDBERG, H. (1983). *The new male-female relationship.* New York: New American Library.

GOULD, R. L. (1978). *Transformations: Growth and change in adult life.* New York: Simon & Schuster.

JOURARD, S. M. (1971). *The transparent self.* New York: Van Nostrand.

JUNG, C. G. (1967). *The collected works of C. G. Jung* (R. F. Hull, Trans.). Princeton, NJ: Princeton University Press.

KAYLOR, J., KING, G., & KING, L. (1987). Psychological effects of military service in Vietnam: A meta-analysis. *Psychological Bulletin, 102,* 257–271.

KEEN, S. (1991). *Fire in the belly: On being a man.* New York: Bantam Books.

KEEN, S., & VALLEY-FOX, A. (1989). *Your mythic journey.* Los Angeles: Tarcher.

KURTZ, R. (1990). *Body centered psychotherapy: The hakomi method.* Mendocino, CA: Life Rhythm.

LEIBMAN, W. (1991). *Tending the fire: The ritual men's group.* Los Angeles: Limbus.

LEVINSON, D. J., DARROW, C. N., KLEIN, E. B., LEVINSON, M. H., & McKEE, B. (1978). *The seasons of a man's life.* New York: Knopf.

LOWEN, A. (1990). *The spirituality of the body.* New York: Macmillan.

MILLER, A. (1981). *The drama of the gifted child.* New York: Basic Books.

MOORE, D., PARKER, S., THOMPSON, T., & DOUGHERTY, P. (1990). The journey continues. In D. Moore & F. Leafgren (Eds.), *Men in conflict* (pp. 277–284). Alexandria, VA: American Association of Counseling and Development.

MOORE, R., & GILLETTE, D. (1990). *King, warrior, magician, lover: Rediscovering the archetypes of the mature masculine.* New York: Harper & Row.

MOYERS, B., & BLY, R. (1990). *A gathering of men* [Videotape]. New York: Mystic Fire Video.

OSHERSON, S. (1986). *Finding our fathers.* New York: Fawcett Columbine.

OSHERSON, S., & KRUGMAN, S. (1990). Men, shame, and psychotherapy. *Psychotherapy, 27,* 327–339.

PECK, M. S. (1978). *The road less traveled.* New York: Simon & Schuster.

RABINOWITZ, F. E., & COCHRAN, S. V. (1987). Counseling men in groups. In M. Scher, M. Stevens, G. Good, & G. A. Eichenfield (Eds.), *Handbook of counseling and psychotherapy with men* (pp. 51–67). Newbury Park, CA: Sage.

RANK, O. (1964). *The myth of the birth of the hero and other writings.* New York: Vintage.

SCHER, M. (1979). The little boy in the adult male client. *Personnel and Guidance Journal, 57,* 537–539.

STEIN, T. S. (1983). An overview of men's groups. *Social Work with Groups, 6,* 149–161.

VAILLANT, G. E. (1977). *Adaptation to life.* Boston: Little, Brown.

WEISS, L., & WEISS, J. (1989). *Recovery from co-dependency.* Deerfield Beach, FL: Health Communications.

WHITFIELD, C. L. (1987). *Healing the child within.* Deerfield Beach, FL: Health Communications.

YALOM, I. (1975). *The theory and practice of group psychotherapy.* New York: Basic Books.

YALOM, I. (1980). *Existential psychotherapy.* New York: Basic Books.

SUGGESTED READINGS

BLY, R. (1990). *Iron John: A book about men.* New York: Addison-Wesley.

BOLEN, J. S. (1989). *Gods in everymen: A new psychology of men's lives and loves.* San Francisco: Harper & Row.

CAMPBELL, J. (1949). *The hero with a thousand faces.* Princeton, NJ: Princeton University Press.

ELIADE, M. (1975). *Rites and symbols of initiation.* New York: Harper & Row.

FIELDS, R., TAYLOR, P., WEYLER, R., & INGRASCI, R. (1984). *Chop wood carry water.* Los Angeles: Tarcher.

FOGEL, G. I., LANE, F. M., & LIEBERT, R. S. (Eds.). (1986). *The psychology of men: New psychoanalytic perspectives.* New York: Basic Books.

KEEN, S. (1991). *Fire in the belly: On being a man.* New York: Bantam Books.

KEEN, S., & VALLEY-FOX, A. (1989). *Your mythic journey.* Los Angeles: Tarcher.

LOWEN, A. (1990). *The spirituality of the body.* New York Macmillan.

MILLER, A. (1981). *The drama of the gifted child.* New York: Basic Books.

PECK, M. S. (1978). *The road less traveled.* New York: Simon & Schuster.

ROGERS, C. (1961). *On becoming a person.* Boston: Houghton Mifflin.

INDEX

Psychotherapy *(continued)*
    common male issues in, 172
    couples, 81
    group, 79, 81, 148, 172
    individual, 81, 172
    men's choice of therapist, 172
Puberty, 16

Rabinowitz, F., 172
Racism, 4
Rape, 99, 100
Relationships, 8, 23–26, 69. *See also* Communication
    ambivalence in male-female, 25
    criticisms of men, 71–75, 81
    differences between male and female, 78
    father-son, 23–26
    fear of commitment in men, 70, 73
    gay, 79. *See also* Homosexuality
    impact of changing work roles, 117
    impact of feminism, 70
    infatuation, 76
    intimacy, 82
    male control of, 72, 82
    male-female, 76–77
    male-male, 78
    male task orientation, 73
    male values, 82
    men and women, 75
    mother-son, 23–25
    similarities between gay and straight, 80
Retirement, 4, 130
Rites of passage, 9, 170, 173
Roe, A., 126
Rogers, C., 45
Romance, 75

Schwarzenegger, A., 141
Self-esteem, 28, 82
"Sesame Street," 4
Sex-machine identity, 97–98
    and ambivalence about sex, 97
Sexual abuse, 94
Sexual fantasy, 95
Sexuality, 7, 93–107, 144
    communication about, 98, 106
    decision making, 103–106
    and emotions, 96
    gay, 102
    male, 93
    male and female approaches to, 100
    myths of, 93
    religious values, 106
    safe sex, 102–103
    sexually transmitted diseases, 104
    traditional masculine values, 144
    women's, 100–102

Sexual orientation, 7. *See also* Heterosexuality, Homosexuality
Smoking, 143
Social support systems, 148
Sorensen, R., 95
Spiritual growth, 169–175
    "descent into the ashes," 167–168
    getting help, 172–174
    and identity, 163, 169
    mythology, 169
Spirituality, 150, 163–164
    and childrearing, 150
    conflicts with traditional male role, 164
    and creativity, 150
    definitions, 164
    and depression, 150
    different pathways, 150
    little boy as metaphor, 165–166
    male spirituality, 164
Stein, T., 172
Substance abuse, 26, 143
Suicide, 47, 52, 141
Super, D., 126

Tannen, D., 10, 77
Task orientation, 44
Telemakhos, 24
Television, 4
Tiedeman, D., 126
Torah, 171
Touch, 55, 99
    hugging and kissing, 99
    misinterpretation, 99
Type A behavior, 47, 143

Values, 124
    career decision making, 124
    and male health, 144
    wellness, 143

Wellness, 145
    emotional, 147–148
    intellectual, 149
    occupational, 148
    personal responsibility, 145
    physical, 145–147
    social, 148
    spiritual, 150
    and values, 145
"Wet dream" (nocturnal ejaculation), 95
Women
    criticisms of men, 70–75
    and relationships, 70
    in the workplace, 24, 34, 117, 119–120, 125, 130
Women's movement, 70
Work, 9, 117–122. *See also* Careers
    and the breadwinner role, 117, 120

PHOTO CREDITS

CHAPTER 1: 1, © 1993 Mickey Pfleger; 9, © Diana Mara Henry, Carmel, CA. CHAPTER 2: 21, © 1993 Mickey Pfleger and Michael Alexander; 30, © Diana Mara Henry, Carmel, CA. CHAPTER 3: 41, © Cleo Freelance Photo; 48, © David Young-Wolff/PhotoEdit. CHAPTER 4: 67, © Michael Siluk; 74, C&W Shields, Inc. CHAPTER 5: 91, © Michael Siluk; 101, © Myrleen Ferguson Cate/PhotoEdit. CHAPTER 6: 115, Courtesy of Honeywell Inc.; 127, © Michael Siluk. CHAPTER 7: 139, © Michael Siluk. CHAPTER 8: 151, © Diana Mara Henry, Carmel, CA; 161, © Michael Siluk; 168, © Michael Siluk.

TO THE OWNER OF THIS BOOK:

We hope that you have found *Man Alive: A Primer of Men's Issues* useful. So that this book can be improved in a future edition, would you take the time to complete this sheet and return it? Thank you.

School and address: _____

Department: _____

Instructor's name: _____

_____

1. What I like most about this book is: _____

_____

2. What I like least about this book is: _____

_____

_____

3. My general reaction to this book is: _____

_____

4. The name of the course in which I used this book is: _____

_____

5. Were all of the chapters of the book assigned for you to read? _____

   If not, which ones weren't? _____

6. In the space below, or on a separate sheet of paper, please write specific suggestions for improving this book and anything else you'd care to share about your experience in using the book.

_____

_____

_____

_____

_____

_____

Optional:

Your name: _____   Date: _____

May Brooks/Cole quote you, either in promotion for *Man Alive: A Primer of Men's Issues*, or in future publishing ventures?

      Yes: _____   No: _____

      Sincerely,

      Fredric E. Rabinowitz
      Sam V. Cochran

FOLD HERE

BUSINESS REPLY MAIL

FIRST CLASS   PERMIT NO. 358   PACIFIC GROVE, CA

POSTAGE WILL BE PAID BY ADDRESSEE

ATT: *Fredric E. Rabinowitz & Sam V. Cochran*

Brooks/Cole Publishing Company
511 Forest Lodge Road
Pacific Grove, California 93950-9968

NO POSTAGE
NECESSARY
IF MAILED
IN THE
UNITED STATES

FOLD HERE